CHAINS TO ROSES

★★★★★

The Joseph Cicippio Story

By

Joseph Cicippio

and

Richard W. Hope

WRS
PUBLISHING

A Division of WRS Group, Inc.
Waco, Texas

First published in the United States of America in 1993 by WRS Publishing,
A Division of WRS Group, Inc. 701 N. New Road, Waco, Texas 76710
Book design by Kenneth Turbeville
Illustrations by Richard Rockwell

10 9 8 7 6 5 4 3 2 1

Library of Congress Cataloging-in-Publication Data

Cicippio, Joseph, 1932-
    Chains to roses : the Joseph Cicippio story / by Joseph Cicippio
and Richard W. Hope.
        p.   cm.
    ISBN 1-56796-025-1 (cloth) : $21.95
    1. Cicippio, Joseph, 1932-   —Captivity, 1986-1991. 2. Hostages—Lebanon—
Biography. 3. Hostages—United States—Biography.
I. Hope, Richard W., 1930-   . II. Title.
DS371.2.K35   1994
956.9204'4'092—dc20
    [B]   93-32205
                                                                   CIP

*This book is dedicated to the memory
of those brave men who lost their lives while being held
hostage in Lebanon:*

—Lt. Col. William Higgins (American)
—William Buckley   (American)
—Dennis Hill   (British)
—Peter Kilburn   (American)
—Leigh Douglas   (British)
—Philip Padfield   (British)
—Alec Collett   (British)
—Michel Seurat   (French)

—Joseph Cicippio

Preface

Beirut was a beehive of stinging violence. Christian Phalangists, Druse militia, Islamic fundamentalists, Sunnis, the Hezbollah (the party of God), Israelis, Syrians—all were locked in bloody combat that would change the face of that once-peaceful land forever.

For Islamics, it was a Jihad, or "Holy War," as proclaimed by fanatical Shia Muslims and relentlessly encouraged by their stern and stoical leader, Ayatollah Khomeini. Brought back from exile in Europe, he would receive a tumultuous reception upon his return to Teheran in 1979. What followed would be a history of events as cruel, murderous, and bloody as the world has ever witnessed.

The raw intensity of Khomeini's mandate allowed no contradiction. You obeyed the Ayatollah or you were thought worthless, and often tortured or assassinated.

These fiery and devoted fundamentalists had no fear of death. Sixteen-year-old girls volunteered to drive vehicles packed with explosives into Israeli convoys. One, Sana Mahaidali, a sixteen-year-old Shiite Muslim, drove a Peugeot 504 chock-full of explosives into an Israeli troop, killing herself and two Israeli soldiers.

In a videotape made before her suicidal mission, she said, "I am very relaxed as I go to do this... because I am carrying out my duty to my people. I hope our souls will form an explosive mixture that will blow up an earthquake on the heads of our enemies."

That fervor, with its explicit and remorseless hatred, has continued to this day. Violent abductions, murder, torture, and cruel imprisonment remain almost daily occurrences in the steaming belly of the Middle East conflict.

Uprooted Palestinians stubbornly resist every effort by Israel to remove them from what they consider to be their holy and rightful homeland. Their hegira to Lebanon—and hopefully to asylum—was met by the burning passions of Christian Maronites, who despised the Palestinians. A new war erupted. The streets and houses and countryside of Lebanon became rich in the blood of both warring factors. The Palestinian Liberation Organization was established to overcome the Christian hegemony. Leftist Muslims demanded the same demographic rights. Dissident organizations sprouted, almost overnight, out of the quickly rubbled streets of Beirut.

The fifteen-year Lebanese Civil War would draw almost every Western nation into the fire of its cauldron. It would also reintroduce to the world an age-old Arab warring practice: the taking of hostages.

None of the hostages could have imagined the fiendish conditions in which they would be held for interminable months and years. British and American hostages, particularly, found themselves pawns to political expedience, misjudgments, and, at times, an almost shrugging indifference to their hellish plights. In retrospect, it can easily be argued that their governments had turned their backs on them. They were on their own, left to face the often blind and senseless hatred of their captors.

Within the context of the Mid-East struggle, it is not difficult to understand why certain key figures were kidnapped: William Buckley was the acknowledged head of the CIA complement in Lebanon. He would die in captivity.

Lt. Col. William Higgins, despite his being an emissary of the United Nations Peace Finding Commission in Beirut, was, after all, a dedicated Marine officer and an American soldier, and therefore automatically suspect. He would be hanged, and his bound, groundless, sandaled feet would be seen turning endlessly on television sets around the world.

But why take a harmless librarian, teachers, an itinerant book salesman, businessmen, a French camera crew, journalists? Were these people who should be held accountable for the slowly dying economy of war-torn Lebanon?

Why take priests and ministers who were there to work selflessly to ease the suffering of people in a very troubled land?

They were American, British, French, or German. In this xenophobic climate, all Westerners were considered demonic by Khomeini. Earlier, Gamal Abdel Nasser had declared an "ethnic cleansing" of Egypt, after he assumed power.

In Lebanon, Westerners were indiscriminately swept off the streets of Beirut: from their places of business, from cafes known to be frequented by high-living Western expatriates, some from their homes or apartments.

One, Frank Reed, a longtime Beirut resident, was kidnapped on his way to a morning round of golf. He was a prosperous local businessman, generous and well admired by the people he had come to know during his eight-year residency in Beirut. He had married a Syrian woman with whom he had a son and had thought himself immune to the factional warfare that surrounded him—a man secure in the eye of a hurricane.

The iron-fisted black hand of the Hezbollah reached out and plucked victims, innocent or not, from the safety of their nests, in order to pursue the cause of Islam, the Holy War, the Jihad. Anything American was (and is) thought of as demonic. The United States is the "Great Satan," a vigorous supporter of Israel, who lends only half-hearted assistance to the rest of the Semite world.

One of those the Hezbollah would kidnap, during a shark-like frenzy of hostage-taking, was a gentle, mild-mannered American, the comptroller of the American University of Beirut.

He had worked tirelessly at the University Medical Center to ease the suffering of wounded soldiers and civilians, of innocent women and children, from every side of the battlements.

On September 12, 1986, he would become a pawn in a cruel game of political blackmail. It would take five years from his life, during which he would endure constant humiliation, relentless tortures, repeated threats to his life, and, perhaps worst of all, painful separation from everything and everyone that he held closest to his heart.

Yet, he would emerge from these almost unimaginable conditions—beatings, hunger, loneliness, rage, and bewilderment—with his soul intact, his spirit renewed. He has become an inspired missionary of love and forgiveness in a world that yearns for salvation.

His name is Joseph Cicippio. This is his story.

Richard Hope
Sag Harbor, New York, 1993

Acknowledgment

The creation of this book was motivated by a single desire—to share with everyone the message that no adversity, however cruel, can overcome the human spirit.

I wanted to express the idea that tragedy can confront any of us at any time in our lives, but that we all possess an inner strength to endure it.

The book would not have been possible without the support of a number of people. James J. "Skip" Oliver, my lawyer and close friend, got the thing going. He found the people needed to make it a reality: Lou Reda of Lou Reda Productions, who creates award-winning films for television; Dr. Wayman Spence, the publisher, who found my story inspiring; Mort Zimmerman, who did valuable research; and three inspired editors, Norman Stahl in New York and Margaret Leary and Georgia Brady in Waco, Texas.

My wife, Elham, provided direction and an attention to detail that was absolutely essential. She had lived through all the terrible years of the fifteen-year Lebanese war and knows more about it than any one of us.

Finally, my friend and collaborator, Richard Hope. We spent many hours putting the story together. And a special thanks to Dan Rather, who wrote a splendid and generous introduction.

—*Joseph Cicippio*
Arlington, Virginia
August 1993

Introduction

In Charles Dickens' *A Tale of Two Cities*, the character of Dr. Manette, after years of unjust imprisonment, is spirited out of the Bastille by supporters who use the password, "Returned to life."

That's just what I thought—they are the words that ran through my head—when I finally saw Joseph Cicippio freed from his unjust imprisonment: Returned to life.

For too long, Joe was kept away from life—from life as we know and understand it. And yet he lived on, leading a life that was not a life, and yet was not a death.

The world went on about its business. Sometimes we thought a lot about Joseph Cicippio and the other hostages in Beirut. But the hostages were not—could not have been—the only story.

There were a lot of stories in those years. Joseph Cicippio missed them.

At CBS News, whenever a hostage was released, we'd prepare a videotape with images from the news events and cultural milestones they'd missed. There were some developments we could only begin to present: I remember Charles Kuralt musing on how best to explain Madonna—and giving up. But we did want to do a little something to bring these remarkable men up to speed.

That little something we did wasn't very much at all.

What we couldn't do, what nobody could do, was to give back to Joseph Cicippio the family picnics, the dinners burnt, the quick hug for no reason in the middle of the grocery store, the late-night arguments, the lazy afternoons curled up with a book, the drives in the country, the smile of somebody else's baby in a stroller on the street, the tears, the laughter, the friends, the loved ones... the private moments that should have made up the years Joe spent in captivity.

What CBS gave Joseph Cicippio was news. That was all we had, and we wanted to give him something. But what Joseph Cicippio needed was life.

Joseph Cicippio was Returned to Life.

This is the story of how that happened.

The life he found is something special.

And if your freedom tastes a little sweeter after reading his experiences, after sharing the freshness and the value Joseph rediscovered, then that's as it should be. His freedom, and mine, and yours are worth rediscovering every day.

—Dan Rather
CBS News

Chapter 1

Joseph: I don't think there was a happier man in the world than I was on the morning of September 12, 1986. I was deeply in love with a beautiful Lebanese woman whom I had married only a year before. We lived in a splendid apartment on the campus of the American University of Beirut (AUB), where I was comptroller. I found my work challenging and exciting. I woke up to another beautiful day. It was everything a man could wish for.

I knew the risks of living in Beirut at that time. There were no real sanctuaries anywhere in that troubled country. The Lebanese Civil War had been going on for over ten bitter years and hostage-taking had been increasing at a frenzied pace. I knew as well that, for some reason, AUB was a particular target.

David Dodge, acting president of the AUB, was the first American hostage taken, in July 1982. He had been brutally treated but was released after a little more than a year of captivity, at which time he warned that the AUB was "the softest target in the whole of Beirut." And he cautioned that he would not be the only hostage taken from the university.

Two years after Dodge was kidnapped, Dr. Malcolm Kerr, who had replaced Dodge as university president, was shot dead outside his office. Peter Kilburn, librarian, David Jacobsen, administrator of the University Medical Center, and Tom Sutherland, acting dean of the AUB School of Agriculture, were all abducted.

David and I were close friends. We had worked hard to improve conditions at the hospital. My door was always open to poor and suffering victims of the war that raged around us. Like me, David had thought himself immune to the terrorists, on some sort of protected list. We thought that because of our humanitarian work at the hospital we would be spared any terrorist act. We were greatly mistaken.

Another close friend was an Englishman, Dennis Hill. We would have breakfast almost every morning at the university cafeteria. Dennis had come to the university to teach and help conduct an English language program for Lebanese students. This enabled many of them to meet the AUB's language requirements. He was abducted near the campus and found with a bullet fired into his head. The Hezbollah, a fanatical group of Islamic fundamentalists, announced that Dennis had been killed while trying to escape. We all knew differently.

There were a lot of aspersions thrown around about Dennis Hill: that he was a womanizer; a heavy drinker; that he had an eye even for some of his female students. But I never saw nor heard any evidence of that until after his death. To me, Dennis was a large, jovial man, extremely bright, who could never do enough for his students. He might have a cocktail at a university party, but I never saw him overindulge. I never saw him make a pass at anyone. He was the model of a perfect English gentleman and scholar, who brought his intellect to the university to give to students—particularly young Lebanese men and women— the store of learning and experience that he had accumulated over the years. Two days after his abduction, he lay dead in the streets of Beirut, a bullet in his brain.

No one could accurately fix the blame or the reason for his execution. The British authorities were willing to accept the charges of Hill's alleged sexual harassment and let it go at that. Westerners in Beirut were relieved, I guess, allowing themselves to believe that as long as they behaved themselves, they would escape any political retribution. But I still think that Dennis Hill was wrongly maligned.

Why he was kidnapped and then murdered is still open to question. Outside of statements made by some Lebanese students at the AUB, many of whom were actively involved in the terrorist underground, there was no evidence that he was anything but the kind and courtly gentleman I remember him to be.

Peter Kilburn, the AUB librarian who was taken in December of 1984, was another close friend. He mysteriously disappeared. No one—not even other hostages who would occasionally be thrown together and hear scraps of news about their fellow captives—ever learned anything of his whereabouts. Peter had simply vanished. Not even his kidnappers, who would normally issue some sort of statement, said anything about him.

I remember Peter as a gentle, soft-spoken man in his mid-sixties, a confirmed bachelor whose only real interest was in the books that lined the walls of his university library. If a student came in and asked for a particular reference piece, Peter was always there to give whatever assistance he could. We had long and pleasant conversations together. Once, he dubbed me "a scholar without portfolio." It pleased me greatly.

I could not imagine why anyone would want to do harm to Kilburn.

One day I got a telephone call from the university staff. Three bodies had been placed in the AUB hospital morgue. Two had been identified as Philip Padfield and Leigh Douglas. They thought the third body might be Alec Collett, a sixty-three-year-old journalist who had worked for the United Nations and whose passport contained a fatal sign: a small, rectangular customs stamp from the state of Israel. At a checkpoint manned by Palestinians, he had been taken from his car at gunpoint. The Revolutionary Organization of Socialist Muslims defiantly claimed responsibility for his abduction. They hanged him some months later in a dispute about seventeen Islamic prisoners held in Kuwait. George Shultz had angrily declared, "The American government is not in the business of negotiating with a bunch of lunatics."

Collett had even appeared in a television tape, some months before, pleading for the release of two Arabs who had been caught while trying to assassinate the Israeli ambassador in Great Britain. It would be a quid pro quo arrangement: Collett's freedom for the Arabs. But the Israelis turned their backs on Collett's plea, as did the British and French Foreign Offices. Collett was left hanging and, ultimately, would be hanged.

I received a second call from the American ambassador, Reginald Bartholomew. He said the embassy had been told that the man lying in the morgue was Peter Kilburn and asked if I would help make a positive identification. The French Embassy persisted in thinking that the man was Alec Collett, and the mystery had to be cleared up.

I thought, Oh no, not Peter. I was shaken, but agreed to do as he asked.

I asked a university professor, William Ward, to accompany me, as much for moral support as anything else. Together we went to the morgue and looked down at the body. He was wearing a jogging suit with a hood, and I asked the attendant to remove it so we could check the color of his hair. I wanted to be absolutely certain, but I think I already knew the worst. It wasn't Collett whose lifeless body I looked down on that day. It was my poor friend Peter Kilburn, his face contorted in some kind of pitiful anguish.

"Yes, that's Peter," I said, and left the morgue.

I walked through the campus for what seemed like hours, thinking that the only crime my innocent friend might have committed was to have been born an American.

Padfield and Douglas were both British. The word around the campus was that they had been killed in retaliation for the bombing of Libya in 1986. The British had allowed American F-111 bombers to be launched from airfields in England. The Libyan leader Muammar Quadaffi's retaliation was to purchase the lives of the three unfortunate men for a considerable amount of money, then have them taken out to a remote beach along the Mediterranean and executed, each in the same way—by a pistol shot behind the left ear.

When I returned to the apartment that night, my wife, Elham, was waiting for me. She saw the terrible pain I was feeling and asked what had happened. When I told her about Peter, we wept together, and once again, she begged me to leave the country. "You must go, Joseph," I remember her saying. "You must leave now before some terrible harm comes to us."

But I was adamantly opposed to leaving. I felt, I suppose in a kind of vainglorious way, that I was somehow special.

I wasn't alone in believing that I was immune to being captured. A number of men who were taken hostage in Lebanon during those years also misjudged the danger. Frank Reed, an American who had built a successful and profitable school in Beirut, was taken off a golf course near the airport. He was married to a Syrian woman and had a child with her. He had converted to Islam, as I had done. He had lived in Beirut for eight years and had enjoyed the friendship and love of his Lebanese neighbors.

Shortly after, rumor began that Frank Reed may have been kidnapped. The American Embassy called me to assist them to confirm the rumor. At that time, the Green Line was closed and few people were able to cross from East to West Beirut. I had quickly sent members of my staff out to check if Frank Reed had been seen by any of his friends or at his school. It became clear very quickly that he was missing. I called the American Embassy to confirm their worst fear.

Still, he would spend almost four years in captivity. When I heard of Reed's abduction, I felt some concern for my own safety, but I continued to think that somehow I had been placed in a special category.

Elham and I were watching the television news when the announcement was made of Reed's kidnapping. They showed a split screen with photographs of four other hostages who had been taken. Their portraits surrounded the screen, but in the middle was an empty space that seemed to ask who would be the next to be taken. Elham felt a shudder of fear. Two other Americans would eventually be taken hostage, Jessy Turner and Robert Polhill—both married to Palestinian women.

Besides my position as university comptroller, I was intensely involved with the AUB Medical Center. David Jacobsen, who was the hospital administrator before he was taken hostage, came to me and asked for help. The hospital was greatly understaffed, he said, and anything that I could do would be welcomed. I tried to chip in. The hospital had only 421 beds, and they were always filled with victims of that senseless war and the many conflicts that surrounded it.

I would look down into the pinched, tear-stained faces of children who could not possibly understand why they should have to endure such agony. Some had lost their entire families in the war. Some had lost an arm or leg. I was determined to help those poor children. I wanted to try to comfort them, to ease their suffering. It was impossible for me to turn away anyone who was in deep financial distress or who needed any kind of physical or moral support. I wasn't heroic or self-sacrificing. I simply did what any concerned human being would do. If you had been there and seen the sad faces of those agonized victims, you would have done the same.

I mistakenly allowed my charitable work to give me assurance that my safety was secure. Lebanese officials had told me again and again that I was in no danger—because of the work I was doing at the university and at the hospital, no one would think of taking me hostage.

When I reminded them that David Jacobsen had been kidnapped and that he had devoted himself even more religiously to the medical center than I had, they said, "Not to worry, Joseph. You are special."

How naive I was. I really believed that, because of my marriage to Elham, my conversion to Islam, my work at the university and hospital, and my great love for the Lebanese people and their country, I was somehow protected from any terrorist attack. I had a kind of gung-ho feeling as well. Despite all the assaults on the campus of the AUB, I thought of myself as Davy Crockett at the siege of the Alamo. I ignored the urgings of the U.S. government and more especially my wife, Elham; I simply would not be moved. I was devoted to the country, the suffering people, to the university and hospital, to Elham and her family, as much as I had ever felt loyalty to anything or anyone. Whatever happened, I was there to stay.

Ego might have been the centerpiece of the table I had set for myself. That, along with the arrogance of believing that maybe I was just a cut above all the rest. But during five years of captivity, I would learn a stern lesson: There is a humility and strength and courage that resides within all of us that needs only to be awakened, a sleeping giant that can help us to surmount any tragedy in our lives.

I admit that I had no such feelings on the morning of September 12. While preparing to dress for her secretarial job at the American Embassy, Elham asked if I would like a cup of coffee. I nodded, and she brought it to the bed where I was lying, feeling like an Eastern potentate. Then she kissed me goodbye and left. In all the years that I was a captive, I never forgot the taste of that coffee and that soft, gentle kiss. Before she left, she reminded me that the next day was my birthday and that she had prepared a special celebration.

When Elham and I were married, I had converted to the Muslim faith, which, I believed, in no way denied my religious upbringing. I was born and raised a Catholic, but I had come to believe that there is one God for all people— Christian, Muslim, Buddhist, or whatever. I would learn that we are all just as grains in the sand, eclipsed by trillions of stars in the heavens.

I believe there are striking similarities between the Islamic faith and Christianity. In fact, if you read the Koran you will find part of the Apostles' Creed replicated almost word for word. This is the one that starts, "I believe in one God, the father almighty, maker of heaven and earth," and so forth. I also believe that those Muslims who commit terrorist acts are in open defiance of their religious teachings, just as the Crusaders were, for example, in the holy wars of the Middle Ages.

In any case, I had no difficulty in converting to the Islamic faith when we were married. In a way I was reaffirming my profound love for Elham. But as we said one last goodbye that morning, neither of us could know that it would be over five long years before we would see each other again. Or that the man leaving the apartment would not be the same man who would be reunited with her so many, bitter years later.

As I left the building, I noticed something odd almost immediately. Normally, there were six to nine guards patrolling inside the building and on the campus grounds. I would always exchange greetings with them, sometimes pausing for a brief chat. This morning they were all strangely missing.

But I quickly dismissed any feelings of uneasiness. It was a beautiful, autumn day in Beirut. The sky was a clear blue. A soft breeze was blowing in off the Mediterranean, and the smell of the multicolored blossoms that lined the campus walkways filled the air.

I thought I was about to begin another exciting day on one of the world's most beautiful campuses. The AUB was, after all, one of the bright stars of learning in the Middle East.

It had been founded by an American, Daniel Bliss, in 1866. He proclaimed it a Western-caliber university that anyone could enter, regardless of their religious beliefs or lack of them. All that was required was a thirst for knowledge and the ability to pass an entrance examination. As such, it attracted students from all over Europe and the Middle East. And when Gamal Abdel Nasser declared an "ethnic cleansing" of Egypt in 1975, it brought to the AUB some of the finest and most vibrant Western educators from the great schools of learning in Cairo and Alexandria. They were also drawn by the high standard of living in Beirut, which was considered to be the Paris and Riviera of the Middle East in the 1960s.

Though many had defected after the beginning of the Lebanese Civil War that same year, the university was still considered to be an outstanding institution, which provided a first-rate education for many thousands of eager students. As I walked down the pathway that morning, I was proud to be a member of it.

I was thinking of what my schedule would be for that morning—completely unconcerned, without the slightest thought of peril. Then, at the end of the path, I noticed three young men engaged in what appeared to be idle conversation. I thought they were students waiting for the early morning classes to begin, and I greeted them cheerfully.

Just as I was passing them, one of them called out my name.

"Mr. Cicippio!"

I turned and they reached out for me. My heart hammering in my throat, I struggled to free myself. Then the butt of a pistol slammed into the back of my head, and the world came crashing in on me.

I slumped forward onto my hands and knees, my vision a blur. I was able to make out my eyeglasses, lying smashed on the pavement and surrounded by drops of blood. When I reached out for them, one of the men kicked them away. A terrorist said, "Don't raise your head or I'll blow it off."

They picked me up and carried me, face down, into a university building and out the other side to an adjacent parking lot. I was then taken to the AUB sea-gate. No guards were present. None of the military men, who normally guarded the gate and prevented anyone suspicious from entering, was there.

I remember watching their scurrying feet and legs as they toted me. I was no easy cargo. I weighed 193 pounds at the time, and I could hear their panting efforts.

I kept thinking they had made a mistake; they had taken the wrong man. But then I remembered that one of them had called me by name. It had been no mistake. Still, I had to cling to whatever hope there was. I tried to convince myself that the Lebanese authorities, the university, perhaps even the U.S. government, would quickly get me released.

They threw me into the rear of a small foreign automobile. A foot pressed down on my neck, pinning my head to the floor of the car. At that point, the events of my entire life passed before me.

The car started off. We drove directly to the Corniche, a road that runs adjacent to the International College, which at one time had housed the British Embassy. Now I could hear the sound of other car engines starting, and I wondered if they were a part of my well-planned abduction.

Finally, I was taken from the lead car and placed into the trunk of another. That happened twice more on our journey. At one point, we paused at a military checkpoint, one of many that had sprung up, impromptu, around the city.

These were manned by Druse militia, Syrians, Christian Phalangists, Hezbollah, or Amal, depending on what part of the city you were approaching. The guards would make some cars pull over, where they would be searched for explosives or other contraband. I prayed that they were friendly and would discover me. But after a few words were exchanged between the guard and our driver, we passed through.

Ultimately, I could hear the sound of aircraft taking off and knew we were somewhere near the airport in Beirut. For a fleeting moment, I thought they might try to smuggle me out of the country. David Dodge had actually been spirited from the country that way and flown to Teheran, never knowing what fate lay in store for him. He was later released in Damascus.

After a while we came to what appeared to be some sort of garage. It was damp and dark and smelled hellishly of car fumes. That place was where I would begin more than five years of cruel confinement, where the tortures of beating and hunger were secondary to those of loneliness, rage, and bewilderment. Maddening boredom alternated with stark terror. I would be totally cut off from my loved ones, never see the sun or stars, never read a newspaper or receive a letter. And for four years of my captivity, I would be chained to a tragic American hostage, whose rapidly deteriorating mental condition often made him an agony to live with.

I could hear the chatter of walkie-talkies as I was ordered from the trunk of the car. I glanced at my captors, saw that they were all masked or hooded and heavily armed with pistols and Kaleshnikov rifles. I would never see their faces nor those of the other terrorists with whom I came in contact through the years.

I was told to take off my clothes, to strip everything off. This humiliation came as a surprise to me, knowing of the Arabs' great embarrassment at nakedness. But with all those weapons brandished at me, I was quick to oblige.

I surrendered my clothing and all my personal belongings: a Cartier wristwatch; my wedding ring, which was precious to me; and five hundred dollars in U.S. currency. I had carried the money for some time in the event that I had to suddenly flee the country. I had thought of it as my "getaway" money, but I never really believed I might someday have to use it. David Jacobsen also did the same.

As one of the guards took my valuables, he said, "Don't worry. These will be returned to you. We are not thieves." I never saw any of my belongings again, although at that moment, I couldn't have cared less. All I wanted was to be free.

They examined my body for what I imagine was CIA material—electronic devices that, of course, I did not carry. I was only a business officer at the university and had no connection with any government agency, but I could never make my captors believe that.

One of them finally brought me a long Arab robe—a *ghalabiya*, that went down to my ankles—and told me to put it on. They opened the trunk of a car and one of them gestured with his AK-47, pointing for me to get in. I got in, curled up in a fetal position, and they closed the lid.

It was strange, but at that moment I felt very calm. Lying there in that almost airless chamber, smelling the foul exhaust fumes, I clung to the idea that it had all been a mistake and that I would soon be released. I tried to reach down into myself to find the strength and courage I would need to endure this terrible experience.

After a while, one of the terrorists opened the trunk lid. "Are you all right?" he asked, in what I thought was almost a kindly way. I nodded, and he told me that we would be leaving soon.

Shortly after, I was put in the back seat of a car. I could hear the engines of what sounded like a fleet of automobiles starting up, then the crackle of walkie-talkies again, and Arabic voices exchanging information.

I was taken to a small house near the airport in a rural part of Beirut. The roads were unpaved and the ruts made the car bounce along noisily. I was relieved when we got to the house and I was carried inside.

They laid out a small mat on the floor of a bare kitchen and told me to lie down and to be silent. Two of them, armed and masked, perched on the kitchen counter and watched me constantly.

I was still bleeding from the blow to my head and drifting in and out of consciousness. But I remember thinking that I would live through this, that I would one day walk again as a free man. I came to know that your mind and body won't let you give up if you are truly determined; that you can live through almost any ordeal, no matter how horrendous, if you are willing to reach deep inside yourself and find the giant within. It was the beginning of my first lesson in survival.

My thoughts were also of my wife, my friends, my family in America. How would they react when they learned that I had been taken hostage? I began to think that if anyone could obtain my release it would be Elham. She is a fiercely determined woman who, faced with impossible odds, would fight until she had surmounted them. And yet she is as gentle and soft and kind as anyone I have ever known. I slept for a while, with her sweet face vivid in my mind and memory.

Chapter 2

Elham: I left for my job at the American Embassy about fifteen minutes before Joseph was to leave. We were so happy together, and I always looked forward to seeing him again when we returned in the evening. We had everything a couple could ask for—work that we both enjoyed, a beautiful apartment facing the Mediterranean, but most important, the sharing of a warm and loving relationship. Still, in my heart, I could not escape the idea that Joseph might be abducted as so many others had been. It often clouded my mind with worry. I warned him many times that he should leave the country, even if it meant that I would be going as well, leaving my family and people. I would have willingly made that sacrifice to keep him safe.

On the morning of September 12, my mind was occupied with many things. I had to renew his passport at the embassy, which I knew would result in all kinds of bureaucratic difficulties. I didn't want Joseph to cross from the university to a photo shop outside the campus, and so we used a photograph that he had had taken previously. That morning I delivered the passport to the consulate's office. I didn't see Joe's passport again until six months later.

I also had his birthday party the next day to think about. I wanted it to be as festive and joyous as anything he could remember, and I had only that day left for preparations. I never expected that he would spend it in captivity.

But Joseph was determined to stay in Lebanon. His work at the university, and especially at the hospital, was very important to him, and he did it tirelessly. Day and night and weekends.

He had grown to love the Lebanese people. His conversion to the Muslim faith was not just because of our marriage. He had told me many times how much he admired the way in which we take care of our old ones and how close our family relationships are, with each looking after the other. He said he had decided years before that if he ever became a convert, it would be to Islam. In many ways, he is as much a Lebanese as I am. But it was because of his work, his faith and dedication, that I had come to believe that Joseph was safe. Lebanese friends of ours, including some local officials, had told us again and again that we had nothing to be alarmed about, and we had believed them. The only precaution he had been told to take was that he should never leave the campus until the struggle was over. Because the university was like a small, charming village, and we had many friends and acquaintances there, this was no real inconvenience.

In fact, Joseph and I had met on the campus at a friend's cocktail party. We were instantly attracted to each other. I was so impressed with his intelligence and his quick sense of humor, but mostly with his kindness and concern for others. He seemed like such a gentle man.

We began a courtship, which was always chaperoned, a tradition in our faith. He met my family and they all took an instant liking to him. Joseph quickly gained their respect and admiration.

Not long after we were married, I remember how joyfully we danced at our wedding ceremony. I would think of it many times in the years that followed.

On that morning of September 12, I had no fears. On my way to the American Embassy, I tried to think of some last, small favor for his birthday party the next day that might please Joseph.

The embassy was no longer the stately official building it had once been in West Beirut. The terrorists had blown that up in April 1983. When the embassy was moved to East Beirut the next year, it was again left in rubble.

Luckily, I missed the first blast, as it had occurred prior to my being hired in April 1983. The second time it was blown, in September 1984, I was recovering from an operation and safe at home. God (Allah) was watching me and saving me for a bigger duty.

But now we worked out of trailers that the U.S.

government had shipped over. They may not have had the prestige of the former establishments, but they were secure, closely guarded, and reasonably safe from terrorist attacks.

We were unusually busy that morning of the twelfth. I was a secretary working in the procurement section. I loved my work and was already deeply involved in my daily routine, when, at 8:30 a.m., I was told there was a phone call waiting for me. It was my brother, Toufic.

"Do you know where Joseph is?" he asked. As soon as I heard Toufic's voice, I felt there was something wrong, for two reasons. First, he never calls so early in the morning. Second, my father was sick. I suddenly asked him what was wrong. It took him a minute to find his words. I felt a tremor in my heart.

"No," I told him, trying to remain as calm as possible. "I left him this morning at the apartment. He was on his way to work."

"Joseph is missing," he said. "Please come to the university at once. Shall I come and fetch you?"

I said I would be there just as quickly as I possibly could. The embassy gave me a car and a driver. Two of my colleagues, Hassan and Souad, volunteered to accompany me. We had to wait for fifteen minutes for an embassy bodyguard to escort us into West Beirut, and then we left for the university.

"Please, hurry," I begged the driver. My heart was beating fast, the palms of my hands were wet. I kept pushing my body forward, trying to urge the car to go more swiftly. I have never seen a car driven as fast as we were. On the half-hour trip to the Green Line, we were almost involved in three accidents, but luckily, the driver was very talented and courageous.

Then we were stopped at the Green Line that separated East from West Beirut. The East was controlled by Christian Maronites, the West by Moslems, and the crossing was often perilous.

Once we arrived at the Green Line, we were left alone, because that was the last crossing point the embassy car was allowed to reach. Luckily, I had my friends. We walked for almost fifteen minutes between cars and trucks until we arrived at the other side. Quickly, Hassen rushed to his car, which was parked somewhere on the edge of the West side, and we drove to the university. We had the radio on hoping to hear any news to contradict our fears, but instead, it was announced that Joseph was missing. All the long way, I was hoping to find Joseph somewhere in one of the many offices at AUB. I simply didn't want to believe. I was repeating the word "mistake." It must be a mistake.

By that time, I was almost hysterical. I lowered my head and folded my hands into my lap, trying desperately to control myself. I prayed. "Please, don't let it be Joseph. Please!"

After what seemed to me a lifetime, we arrived at the university where I was taken directly to Joseph's office. It seemed so empty and cold. No one there offered me any information. It seemed as if they were all afraid to talk to me.

When I left the office to find someone to tell me what had happened, I met my brother. He took my arm gently and led me to the police, who wanted me to make a statement.

"Elham," an officer said. "Do you know where Joseph is? He hasn't arrived at the office this morning."

My hands twisted nervously. How could I know where he was? I had last seen him at the apartment that morning. They turned their faces from me in a kind of embarrassed sympathy. They already knew what I, in a kind of desperation, still refused to admit to myself. There was an empty silence in the room.

My brother, Toufic, laid his hand gently on my shoulder. "Come, Elham," he said. "They want to talk to you at the apartment."

We crossed the campus together. Near the apartment building I saw a large group milling around, thrusting microphones into the faces of people I couldn't recognize, taking photographs, wielding cameras. I looked down at the pavement, not wanting to believe what was happening, and there I saw Joseph's eyeglasses, smashed to the ground with a spattering of blood surrounding them. I picked the broken glasses up and put them into my purse. Not until that moment was I truly convinced that he had been taken hostage. Later, I tried to place his eyeglasses over my eyes, just to be able to see the last scene Joseph had seen. It was stupid, but I did it.

The media people shouted questions at me as we entered the building, but my throat was too full of tears to answer them. I don't remember what I said. They trailed into the apartment where my brother led me into the bedroom. There he and my father tried to console me, but I was inconsolable.

Joseph was gone.

My brother tried as best he could to handle the onslaught of reporters and cameramen. We all knew that Joseph had been kidnapped. However, the group that had taken him would not announce it until a week later in one of the local newspapers. By that time, it had become a major news event.

The media people went rummaging through our apartment as though they lived there. One even asked Toufic if he could borrow a wedding picture of Joseph and me that hung just inside the front doorway. Toufic said, "I don't know, I'll have to ask my sister." When he looked back a while later, the picture was gone. The reporter was gone. We would see the photo later, in the press, cut in half, showing only Joseph without me beside him. It was just the beginning of a number of small cruelties that people would inflict on us in the years to come. But, of course, they were nothing compared to the terrible suffering Joseph would have to endure.

I felt I was the last person to be asked for testimony. I felt so miserable and without any support. Yet I had to answer all the questions. I can still clearly remember the questions that the Lebanese police asked me that night. "Do you know what he was wearing?" I didn't know how to answer even this question. "Tell us how he was kidnapped!" "How many people were waiting to kidnap him?" "From where was he taken?" Hundreds of questions. In fact, he was asking me the same questions I wanted to ask him. Finally, he did tell me, "We have located a janitor who saw two men trying to carry your husband. He had rushed to them thinking they were carrying someone to the hospital. He said they locked him with the gate guard at the sea gate with a pistol at their heads. He couldn't describe the kidnappers."

After all of their interrogation, they asked me to sign a statement, which I did, not really knowing what was on it. Nor did I care. All I knew was that Joseph was in a place where I could not reach him.

For the next three days I had no sleep, no rest. I would go out onto the apartment balcony, hoping to see a car pull up and Joseph emerge. I would look at photographs of us and remember the wonderful moments we had spent together. For a while I set a place for him at the breakfast or dinner table, hoping he would miraculously arrive. But the plates stayed empty, the cups unfilled.

Since the very first day, the phones had never stopped ringing. Reporters wanted to ask me what I thought about the kidnapping, what I was going to do, if I would remain in Lebanon. The hardest question I was ever asked was, "How do you feel, Mrs. Cicippio?" I simply couldn't take that question. In what way could I explain how I felt? There weren't any words to explain the insecure and miserable position I was put in. Although the situation in Beirut at that time was critical, I never even considered leaving the country—the country where my poor husband was being held. They weren't interested in making Joseph a free man, they were only interested in making a sensational news story at our expense. My expense or Joseph's, his family's or friends'. I decided to fight back, to wage a war of my own to get my husband released. That was my passion. It was to fill my hours for years to come.

I tried to reach everyone who might know something about Joseph—where he was being held, who was holding him, what I could do to bring him home to me. Always I got blank stares, sad, half-smiling, empty faces. Go home, Elham, they would say. Go home, there is nothing you can do.

I refused to believe it. You have to understand, I wasn't trying to be a heroine. I simply wanted my husband back.

My brother, who was generally scornful of such things, had been told by a friend of his that there was a gifted spiritualist, a man who could tell us where Joseph was and how we could obtain his freedom.

I was grasping at any small shred of hope, and so I traveled through a rubbled, war-torn area of West Beirut to meet him at his squalid home. There was a single light hanging from the ceiling, but otherwise the room was barren and cold. We sat on the top steps of the stairs. He took my hand and seemed to go into some sort of trance. "Yes, Elham," he said, "I know where your husband is and I can make him free."

He told me it would take twenty-five thousand dollars to release my husband from the people who had taken him. I offered ten thousand, as a kind of down payment. It was all I could raise.

He refused. He said he had to have the whole amount or nothing. I told him I would think about it, but, as I left his house, I realized how foolish I was to think that some self-proclaimed mystic might have our destinies in his hands. But I also thought of Joseph, and I was tempted to try to do anything that might set him free, to be with me again.

A stream of people began to come with promises to get Joseph released. They called me on the telephone. One even came to the door of our apartment. They all said they knew where Joseph was and who was holding him. For a certain amount of money they would arrange for his freedom. I felt that I had no choice but to take part in this gambling game. But, of course, I never heard from any of them again. Losing the money wasn't the cruel part. I would do it again. It was the empty promises that shattered my hopes time after time.

I realized that those people knew no more than I did about the terrorists who were holding Joseph. The group that had taken him was apparently too well-organized and heavily financed. They didn't need the modest sums I was able to raise. And, in any case, it seemed impossible to approach them.

I never gave up hope. I continued to meet with anyone, everyone, I thought could help me. Then I learned the name of the group who had kidnapped my husband. It was the Revolutionary Justice Organization, a very radical group who had close ties with the Islamic Jihad. I discovered that they were Iranians who were unhappy with the West and had decided to strike out on their own.

When they released photographs of Joseph, I was saddened to see how poor Joseph looked. But at least I knew he was alive.

Shortly after, I called Terry Waite, who had acquired some international fame by obtaining the release of a few British hostages some time before. I agreed to meet him, along with Jean Sutherland and Fifi Reed, the wives of two other hostages, at the Riviera Hotel to find out if there was anything he could do to free Joseph.

Though I had hoped for a small, private meeting, he insisted on my joining him in the hotel lobby, where we could be photographed together. I was surprised at the presence of all the media and not very happy about it, but I agreed. He said it would show the world that he was working for the hostages. What that had to do with Joseph, I didn't know.

I was not very impressed with Terry Waite. I thought he was a vain man, more interested in himself than in the hostages. He told us he was trying to arrange a meeting with the Islamic Jihad to obtain the release of Thomas Sutherland and Terry Anderson. He was only partly successful, in that, not long after we spoke, the Jihad made him a hostage as well. Terry Waite would not, as he had hoped, become *Time* magazine's "Man of the Year."

Terry Waite's capture was one more time that I despaired. I would recall how strong Joseph was, though, how pure he was inside, and that is what kept me going for all those years. I would never surrender my faith, my belief that one day Joseph and I would be together again.

Chapter 3

Joseph: Late on the first day of my captivity, the guards shook me awake. I think it was after midnight. They led me to the bathroom, where I was allowed to wash away the blood from my head wound and to use the facilities. The room had been filled with insects, which had bitten and stung me and left marks all over my body. It had become so bad that they removed me to the house next door, where I was to remain for several weeks.

The guards seemed to take little interest in me, although they watched me constantly. I would hear them chattering in Arabic as I lay on the floor of the living room. I never saw their faces. Either I was blindfolded, which was a good part of the time, or they wore dark masks and hoods. If I were to meet one of the terrorists today, I could not possibly recognize him.

Since the morning of my abduction, I had been given no food, only a small drink of water. But now, on this second day, they brought me a small dish of jelly, a slice of bread, and some dark Turkish coffee. I was grateful.

I noticed that the food was served on dishes with a TWA insignia—even the silverware was TWA's. I recalled the TWA hijacking in 1985, when a group of Shia terrorists had taken a plane that was headed from Athens to Rome and forced the pilot to fly all across the Mediterranean before landing at the airport in Beirut.

They had demanded the release of seventeen Dawa prisoners who had been captured after a suicide attempt on the motorcade of Sheikh Jaber, the ruler of Kuwait. He escaped only because the Shia driver of a car loaded with explosives had missed his target. Two bodyguards, a passerby, and the driver were killed in a blast that echoed throughout the city of Kuwait.

The passengers on the plane, many of them Americans,

couldn't understand why the terrorists were running up and down the aisle shouting, "New Jersey! New Jersey!" That was because the battleship *New Jersey* had shelled the Lebanese coastline only about a year before.

I remembered a television news broadcast that showed a terrorist leaning from the cockpit window. He was holding a gun to the pilot's head and shouting demands to people on the ground.

Later the terrorists took a young Navy Seal, shot him, and threw his body to the tarmac. It was an awful thing to see, but even worse was when they brought the young man to the AUB Medical Center. I was there and saw his lifeless body wheeled in on a gurney. The young sailor—whose name was Robert Stethem—was a totally innocent victim of a war that seemed to have no boundaries.

As I finished my supper, I began to realize that the people who had taken me were no ordinary terrorists. They were a trained, well-organized, fanatical group, who would not hesitate to execute me if they thought it might further their cause.

That thought came immediately to my mind when, not long after I had been kidnapped, a guard came into my room and told me that I would be tried in absentia. The jury would weigh everything they knew that was good about me and everything that was bad. That's just the way he put it.

It was what we call, in America, a kangaroo court. I was powerless to do anything except await whatever verdict they came up with. They had absolute control over my life. Except through my steadfast prayers, there was no higher court to which I could appeal.

In the room where I was being kept, I imagined myself facing a Draconian judge who had already decided I was guilty and doomed. I would persuade him that I loved the Lebanese people, that I had worked tirelessly on their behalf. That I was a Muslim and had a Lebanese wife. That I was not CIA, an agent. That my closest ties were with Lebanon, the university, and the medical center. Oh, how eloquent I was in my imagination! The judge would be reduced to repentance, the jurors' heads bowed and chastened. The judge would rise and say, "Mr. Cicippio, we have made a grave error. You are free to go home to your family." How sweet fantasies can be when we indulge in them. They can nourish us and lull us to sleep, always believing that tomorrow will be better.

But my conscious mind had begun to awaken to reality. I began to realize that only by reaching deeply within myself could I find the wellsprings of strength that could help me to survive or even to endure whatever fate might be in store for me and so, I began to mentally and spiritually prepare. I began to build a fortress around myself that no indignity, no humiliation, no cruel treatment could ever penetrate.

I would never know if I was absolved in their strange court of justice. But since I wasn't executed, I presume I did all right. Most likely, it was because I was useful to them. A dead hostage isn't worth much.

Then the interrogations began, and they were brutal.
Three or four of the guards would suddenly, without any
warning, burst into the room where I was kept. One of
them would blindfold me, and then they would drag me
into another room, where I would be forced to kneel, my
head bowed. Two of them would wrench my arms behind
me and I would remain in that painful position all through
the questioning.

The interrogator's voice wasn't familiar to me. It wasn't
one of the guards, so I figured it was someone from the

outside, a higher official in the organization.

He would begin softly, asking my name. I would answer,
"Joseph Cicippio." Then his voice would take on a sterner
and more menacing tone.

"How long have you been CIA?"

"I am not CIA."

"Don't lie! If you lie, we will kill you!"

I knew, of course, that if I admitted any complicity with the CIA, I would have a very short time to live. In any case, I was telling the truth.

"You're an agent. Tell us!"

"No. I'm just an accountant at the university. The comptroller."

"Yes. A nest of spies. We know it and you know it. Tell us!"

The men holding my arms wrenched them back even

harder, and they pushed me down until my forehead almost touched the floor.

I told them the university depended mostly on private donations, and that we were constantly fighting the red ink. Without the annual grants from the United States

Agency for International Development, the university would not have been able to continue operating. I wanted to tell them as much as I could without putting anyone in jeopardy. My inquisitor would pause and then begin a new round of questions.

"Why have you remained in Lebanon when so many others have left?"

"I love the Lebanese people. My job is here. I am married to a Lebanese woman. I am not CIA!"

The questioning seemed to take forever and would continue from time to time for the next few months. Always they would drag me back to my pallet and leave me there, breathless and close to tears, but grateful that I had survived another interrogation.

They would continue interrogating me, though, and in even crueler ways. I would be taken, blindfolded, and forced to kneel on the floor once again. They would bark a salvo of questions at me, always about any involvement of mine with the CIA.

I would hear the chilling click of a single cartridge thrust into the chamber of a revolver. "Now tell us," they would say. "Tell us about the CIA. Tell us what your job is there."

I had nothing to tell them, of course, and would plead my innocence. Then I would hear the spinning of the cylinder, and feel the cold touch of a gun barrel pressed against my temple.

"I have nothing to do with the CIA," I would say. "I can't tell you anything." I would hear the snap of the revolver and wince each time, expecting to be instantly blown away.

"Tell us what you know or you're a dead man," the voice would say. I would insist I knew nothing.

Again, the spinning of the cylinder, the barrel pressed to my temple, the snap of the trigger. I could hear guards in the background tittering, amused by this exquisite torture. On one occasion they did this procedure seventeen times. I counted every click.

But after a while it became almost tedious. I knew they didn't want me dead. A live hostage was someone they could barter with.

This cruel game of Russian roulette was not the only

torment my captors visited on me. Some of the places in which I was held were teeming with vermin—rats, mice, insects of every kind. I could feel the bugs crawling over my body at night, and in the morning I would awaken with bites from head to toe, as if the creatures had been trying to devour me.

When I pleaded with the guards to do something, anything, they captured a particularly large and ugly insect and lit a match to it. They explained that its odor was a repellent that would drive off the other insects. The smell was almost as bad as the bites.

Whether they were toying with me, enjoying my agonizing discomfort, I can't say. But in a few days they moved me to another location. It was a bombed-out building just a short distance away.

Any idea of mine that I would be treated more kindly soon vanished. I was put into a cramped shower stall that was dark and windowless. I thought it would be for only a short time, until they were able to find a space for me, but when night came I realized that this was my new home.

I don't think I had ever felt as alone and desolate as I did in that cramped, airless chamber. I kept tossing and turning at night, trying to find a comfortable position in which to sleep.

In a way, that purgatory of confinement turned out to be almost a blessing. I was alone, most often in darkness. I could easily have spent those hours and days railing against the cruelty of my captors, filling myself with bitterness and hatred.

Instead, I began to learn that the anger and hatred I carried would surely exhaust me. I remembered reading that there are more stars in the heavens than in all the grains of all the sands of the earth; that looking to the heavens was more profitable than dwelling on the situation on earth. Where had I been, after all, when the stars first shone? It was an humbling thought, but one that helped to sustain me through the rest of my captivity, and does even to this day. Though I was deprived of even the smallest glimpse of the heavens, I kept my vision upward. Hatred, I came to believe, was not the answer to anything.

Forgiveness, however, was a harder philosophy to maintain. When I thought of my wife, Elham, left alone, I sometimes felt rage and sadness. What was she thinking? What was happening in her life?

I thought of my family in America.

There were times during my captivity when I felt completely forgotten by the outside world.

I was sure that Elham would do anything she could to get me released. I was certain that my family would exert every effort to bring me home. I was not so sure of the U.S. government, the university, or the changing geo-political nature of the wars that were raging in the Middle East. My suspicions were to be confirmed.

I later learned that the United States had declared an iron-bound policy of never dealing with the hostage-takers.

The British, the Israelis, the French, all capitulated to Washington's mandate, although the French became somewhat skillful in sidestepping the rules.

But where did that leave me and the other hostages? We were all men at the peak of our lives, doing the things we were best suited for, enjoying our families and friends, and the clean, fresh air of freedom.

I think most of us take those things for granted. I will always cherish the freedom to simply pick up a newspaper or magazine, switch on the radio or television, take a short stroll or a brief spin in the car with my wife, if we decide to. But the door had suddenly been shut on those ordinary pleasures, and I was a captive. Everything that I had ever loved, everything I had known, everything that had filled my life with hope, had stopped dead in one day. Here I was in a cold, dark, and empty world.

Strangely, something in me ignited an almost spiritual will to survive. In the lonely confinement of that bathroom stall, I began to review my past in what I believe was a painstakingly honest way. I was the youngest of nine working-class children in a family whose parents had migrated to America from Italy in 1911. We were a family filled with love, and I cherish every moment that we were all together. But I had become restless.

I had wanted to go out and prove myself, to become an inspired example of the American dream. I worked part time from the eighth grade on, but still managed to graduate from high school. I then went on to college, the first in my family to do so. It wasn't because I was smarter than they were. It was simply because my brothers and sisters had had to work long hours to keep the family together. They willingly sacrificed their early education in order for us to have food on the table. As the youngest, I was pampered.

There were twenty-eight thousand people in Norristown, Pennsylvania, where we lived, but I feel as though I got to know every one of them. I was a drummer in the high school marching band and with the Veterans of Foreign Wars. I thought about trying out for the high school baseball or football teams, but I just didn't have the time for it. I did, however, become a member of the school Historian Club. I enjoyed that. The American Civil War particularly interested me. There was no way I could have imagined that one day I would be involved in another civil war as far from Norristown, Pennsylvania, as my mind could reach. When I was thirteen years old, I thought of the Middle East as a fascinating place where endless caravans moved slowly through drifting desert sands. Movies like *Four Feathers* and *Algiers* filled my youthful imagination with a very romantic notion of what that remote part of the world was truly like. I could not have dreamed that someday it would become a very important part of my life.

After high school, I went to work as a teller at the People's National Bank of Norristown, Pennsylvania. I attended banking programs at night for about ten years at the University of Pennsylvania, Villanova University, and the Stonier Graduate School of Banking at Rutgers, earning a number of banking diplomas. I was made manager of the bank's East Norristown office in 1963. I like to think that I had gained the affection of local small businessmen who were seeking loans. There were times when I lent them money from my own pocket, even before the necessary documents were executed. I was active in all the local service organizations that I thought would help people: the March of Dimes, the Boy Scouts, the United Way. I'm sure it sounds boastful, but I was ready to do whatever I could to provide help for anyone I thought needed it. It was the way I had been brought up. My parents had always told us to reach out a hand to anyone less fortunate than ourselves.

But there was a dark side to my ardor. I devoted many hours away from my family, time I should have been spending with my children. I went through two difficult marriages, both to women I admire. I confess that my workaholism was the major reason for the difficulties. Now, in captivity, I was able to dwell on repairing the mistakes that had, in many ways, driven me to the Middle East.

In that dark and lonely place I was able to say, "Look, this is the old Cicippio. If I ever come out of this alive, I will be a new person, even more deeply devoted to my wife and family and all the people around me."

I think it was a Greek philosopher who said simply, "From suffering comes wisdom." It was a thought I would come to learn the meaning of even more profoundly in the years to come.

After I had spent three days in the shower stall they came to move me once more. I was bound and blindfolded, taken outside, and led to another automobile where I was pushed into the trunk. I remember thinking that anything would be an improvement over my last confinement. I was wrong.

I was driven to the building I had previously been in and then, shortly after, taken to the house next door. I would remain there until November 4, 1986. And it was there that I would be united with a fellow hostage. We would be together for the next four-and-a-half years.

One night I heard the sounds of a terrible beating in the room next door. I could hear the shouted questions of the terrorists as they mercilessly interrogated some helpless victim, the muffled sound of the blows that rained down on his body, the piteous cries as he begged them to stop. "Please," he cried, "you're killing me. You're killing me! Oh, God, help me! Save me!" And then the drumfire of questions would resume, the sound of blows, his agonized protests. It filled me with deep sadness. And the fear that I was the next one to be treated so brutally.

But then one of the guards came into my cell and told me not to worry. "The man is a German thug," he said. "He refuses to obey and deserves no pity." But I had heard the man's voice and knew that he was an American.

The beatings continued for the next few weeks, and I would cover my ears to shut out the unbearable sounds of his misery. And then one night the man was brought into my cell. He was tall and well-built, with a shock of snow-white hair.

His name was Edward Austin Tracy, and he was an international bookseller, who had been sipping coffee at his favorite West Beirut cafe when the terrorists came and swept him out of his seat and half-carried him to a waiting automobile. There could have been no reason to abduct him except that he was an American.

What the kidnappers didn't realize was that this poor tragic man was already in the beginning stages of a severe

mental disorder. His aberrant behavior in captivity was the
reason he had been treated so brutally. It wasn't until his
captors finally understood that Edward was in severe mental
distress that the beatings stopped.

The first time I saw Tracy, I noticed the vague, distant
stare in his eyes. He muttered constantly to himself. I think
Tracy never truly understood the situation we were in, and
while he would add to the daily torture of my confinement,
I have nothing but the greatest sympathy and regard for the
man. He would have to endure the same torment of beatings,
hunger, and vile confinement that all the hostages were
subjected to. But he would never actually understand what
was happening to him. Of course, his mental condition
grew rapidly worse.

It was late at night when he was led into my cell. He was

ordered to sit on the floor, facing me, and we were both cautioned not to say a word to each other.

I wondered about this man who seemed so totally ravaged by his experience. I listened to his pathetic murmurings and wondered what his inner voice was saying to him. Finally, I took the risk of talking to him.

"What's your name?" I asked, in the softest voice possible.

"Tracy," he replied. "Edward Tracy."

"American?"

"Yes, from Vermont."

"My name is Joseph Cicippio," I said. "I'm American, too. Don't let them get you down, Edward. We'll come out of this all right."

And then he returned to his inner voices again. I thought how fortunate I was not to be so mentally disfigured, and I

determined, once again, to find a way to keep my mind and my soul intact. I resolved that, with God's help, I would survive.

It was after midnight when the guards came in and told us we were going to be moved. We were squeezed into the trunk of a car and driven a short distance to yet another site. I prayed that I wouldn't be taken back to the shower stall, but this is one time that I almost wished my prayers hadn't been answered.

The terrorists took us to a high-rise apartment building somewhere in Beirut. It was twelve stories high, which I knew because we were made to trudge up every weary flight and I counted them all. Like every other time I was moved, I could not escape the idea that this might be my final destination; that they had decided I was no longer of any use to them and that killing me would be the easiest solution.

Then one of the guards poked me with the barrel of his assault rifle. "Keep your head down," he demanded. "Don't look up." His words were almost encouraging. I realized that if they didn't want me to recognize this new place of captivity, they might have some further use for me.

"Move! Move!" they kept saying as we ascended the stairs. I went as fast as I could. At last we got to the top landing, panting and exhausted from the effort. Our captors, most of whom were in their twenties, were breathing hard as well.

I had only a brief look at the modest apartment we were taken into before we were shoved across the room and onto an outdoor balcony. Here we were given a pair of flimsy blankets and told to lie down on thin, foam-rubber mats placed on the concrete floor.

Again, I assumed that we would be kept there for only a short time until they could arrange something more suitable for us. Again I was painfully mistaken. As fragile and tenuous as our existence was, our masked and hooded captors had no intention of making it easier for us. For whatever reason, they expected us to suffer.

The balcony had a makeshift cinder-block wall, which rose about eight feet and was piled with sandbags that totally obscured the sky. The walls of the building were pockmarked with bullet holes, a reminder of the bitter war that continued to rage around us.

There was nothing we could do about the icy winter wind that came howling, day and night, through the sandbags and the hastily built walls. We were wearing light running suits and had only flimsy blankets to ward off the cold.

At night, the floors and walls of the balcony were often rimed with frost, and I soon despaired of trying to sleep. My sad friend, Tracy, lay under his ragged blanket, murmuring unintelligibly, moaning and sometimes crying out. Still, seeing him lying there, I sometimes wished I could escape into the sad world he was wandering through. There were times when I thought about death, an end to the suffering. But then, one night, pacing the floor of the balcony, shrouded in my thin blanket and trying desperately to keep

warm, I came to a sudden realization. Who was I to feel pity for myself? What was my suffering compared to Edward Tracy's or to millions of other people's? I was only an infinitesimal part of the cosmos, a tiny grain of sand, greatly

outnumbered by all the glittering stars in the heavens. Though I couldn't see the night sky, my inner vision once again turned upward.

In Zen Buddhism there is the concept of the empty rice bowl. If the rice bowl is full, the universe cannot fill it. In my distress, I determined to clear my mind of every thought, save for my family and loved ones, to empty my "rice bowl." It was an epiphany for me. Walking that dark balcony, shivering against the night wind, I began to create what would be a different person than the man who had been taken only months before.

Certainly, the transformation has been no easy ambition to realize. But it further strengthened me to endure the months and years that lay ahead. I continue to work at it, and admit that I am not always successful in curtailing a certain amount of bitterness. Especially when I recall those desperately cold nights on a balcony in Beirut, when I was too frightened to sleep for the fear that I would never awaken. However, I came to understand that once I had forgiven my captors, I was no longer a victim.

I suffered permanent frostbite of my hands and feet during the three months we were kept on that frigid balcony. I still often feel painful discomfort, as though fiery needles are being stuck into my bones. But I have no hatred for my captors. They were doing what they thought was just. They were innocent pawns caught up in a war that had swept so many of their own people away.

I prayed, of course, kneeling on the cold, concrete floor of the balcony, but it seemed, at times, as though my pleas for some kind of deliverance would never be answered.

Then one day in early February, I heard the angry protests of a man whose voice I did not recognize. He was obviously a higher official in the Revolutionary Justice Organization. He had seen the mean conditions in which we were being held and was beside himself with anger. The people who were holding us sounded as if they were making mild and mumbled protests, but each apology was met with a tirade even more vocal than the last. I didn't need to know Arabic to understand that our guards were being severely chastised. My only worry was that the guards would take out their frustrations on us.

The next day, an army of them came out to whitewash the walls and shore up the cracks where the winter winds relentlessly blew. I thought I recognized one of the men, even though he was hooded, as the guard who had come out on the balcony soon after we arrived in that place of captivity, and who had said to us, "Don't do anything to create trouble. You know, the guards here can kill you anytime they wish." I was not about to disbelieve him.

During the three months that Tracy and I spent on that balcony, I had never endured such misery. Although Hell is thought of as a place of fire and sulphur and interminable heat, there were times that I thought I might willingly exchange our balcony for it, rather than try to exist in that cold and desolate place.

Misery, the old saying goes, loves company, but I had none save for my poor fellow sufferer, and he was lost in a world I hope never to travel. The endlessly long hours on the balcony gave me precious time to think, however, to rearm myself against any cruelty my captors might decide to inflict. Brick by brick, I was beginning to build a fortress around myself that no indignity could ever penetrate, no suffering could overcome.

On February 9, 1987, we were moved to another house not far from the apartment building. We were blindfolded, as usual, and put in the trunk of an automobile. But by this time I had learned how to travel in that bizarre manner. I would curl up as comfortably as possible, breathe deeply and evenly, and remain silent. There were times when these trips were almost restful.

We arrived at the new location about four o'clock in the morning and were taken to a small room on the fourth floor of the building. Once again, I counted every step and landing. It was a way, I suppose, of keeping my mind active. Simple but effective. I can remember the dates of every instance in which I was moved from one place to another, almost to the hour. I know that there were 107 sandbags on the balcony. Without any other diversions, not a newspaper or magazine, these small mental exercises helped to make the long, tedious hours of captivity a little more bearable. I was determined to keep my mind as active as possible.

While we were in that house, I could hear the voices of other Americans in an adjoining room. One of them seemed to be very ill. I tried to imagine who they were. My friend David Jacobsen might have been one—perhaps Terry Anderson, Tom Sutherland, or Frank Reed. But I couldn't make out their identities from their muffled voices. How I wished I could meet with them, if only for a few moments. But for some reason, my guards never allowed me to meet any American hostage other than Edward Tracy.

Edward Tracy and I would sit quietly listening to their voices and soon realized the Americans in the next room were professors from Beirut University College taken hostage less than a month before. Although we shared the same toilet with them, Tracy and I were forced to face the wall as they passed through our room to the toilet.

The sound of the sick hostage, though, filled me with concern. I remembered how poorly William Buckley had been treated, before ultimately dying in captivity.

Everyone in Beirut had known that Buckley was the local CIA chief and a natural target of the terrorists. The Hezbollah released three videotapes of Buckley while he was being held. The cassettes were mailed to the U.S. Embassy in Athens and were particularly gruesome.

The first had no sound and showed Buckley naked on a bed and being beaten, while clutching some sort of document to his stomach.

In the next he was shown—his arms and legs shaking spasmodically—pleading to his government to remove all American and Israeli influences from Lebanon.

In the last video, he stammered a prepared statement that praised his captors and demanded Lebanon's right to rule its own destiny. Buckley was emaciated and his arms were marked with puncture wounds, which suggested that he had been drugged.

David Jacobsen later told me that he could hear Buckley's constant, wracking coughs from the room next to his. David had pleaded with the guards to help the suffering man, but they did nothing.

At one point, David heard Buckley, who was in a state of delirium, say to one of the guards, "I'll have my hot cakes with blueberry syrup now." Shortly after, he heard the sound of feet moving down the corridor. Buckley was dead and they were removing his body.

One of the guards later said to Jacobsen, "He is in a wonderful place now where the sun is shining and the birds are chirping." David wondered, somewhat cynically I imagine, why, if they really believed that version of heaven, they didn't all just end it for themselves. Occasional bitterness came naturally to most hostages, especially in moments of sorrow, despair, or depression.

I foolishly thought that the worst that could happen, short of death, was behind me. What could fill me with greater terror than being forced to kneel in a painful position before a faceless interrogator, and be repeatedly threatened with death? Or having to endure their sinister game of Russian roulette? Once they had even stripped my trousers down, pressed the sharp point of a knife against my genitals, and told me I would be castrated if I didn't tell them what they wanted to hear.

Even those terrifying moments seemed almost pale when compared to the desperate loneliness I had felt in the cramped confines of a shower stall or the terrible ordeal of three months on the icy balcony of a high-rise building. I had been threatened with death repeatedly, but I had never quite taken the threats seriously. Even when the guards had

become enraged at Edward's incessant rantings and said they would shoot us both if he didn't shut up, I didn't think they would carry out the threat. Lined up, facing the wall of the balcony, I was almost calm. What would they do with two dead hostages? And what could I do about Tracy? It was far more painful for me than for the guards to have to listen, day and night, to his piteous cries.

On February 10, 1987, we were shown a television report announcing that unless 254 Palestinians were released from Israeli prisons, many hostages would be put to death. For the first time I had the cold feeling that they had every intention of carrying out their threat. I remember seeing the Israeli prime minister smiling and waving from the back of a U.S. gunboat, and for the first time I felt some enmity toward their government. It seemed as though they had no concern about the plight of the hostages, and I would discover, later on, that I was not altogether mistaken.

I lived each day expecting that at any moment my captors would come into the room and whisk me off to my execution site. I began to prepare myself for death. I mentally wrote letters to my wife and family, knowing they would never receive them, but hoping that in some way they would understand the feelings I had for them.

On some days a guard would come in and tell me, "Not today, Cicippio, not today." Those taunting words always reminded me that tomorrow no words at all would deliver a more chilling message.

The threat was lifted when the United States, in a show of strength, sent warships into the port of Haifa. I was totally exhausted by the ordeal and deeply depressed. I had already realized that my life had little value to the terrorists, but now I began to think that it didn't matter all that much to my own country. They had sent warships to ports in Israel, but what were they doing to negotiate for the freedom of American hostages, or any of the hostages for that matter? Once again I heard the defense secretary's iron-bound edict, "No dealing with terrorists." I thought that if the Western nations' position was going to be so inflexible, there was no way any of us would ever be released.

For a while it did appear that not only would my life be spared, but that Tracy and I would actually be released. We were told by one guard that we would be freed if one of two things happened. One was if the battleship *New Jersey* returned to shell the Lebanese coastline as it had done in 1984.

Two things had triggered that event: the destruction of the American Embassy in 1983, and the suicide truck bombing of the American and French military barracks in Beirut the same year. The battleship fired two hundred sixteen-inch shells at what they called rebel positions in the Chouf Mountains, but the shells did very little damage. That was the end of U.S. "gunboat diplomacy." Still, there was no question that the ship could do considerably more damage.

The other condition that would have freed us was the release of the Palestinian prisoners. But Israel was adamant on that score even though the Israelis could have quadrupled the number of men they were holding. They could have released the 254 and gone right out and taken the same number in no time. But it was no go, and Tracy and I sadly took off our "freedom" clothes and got back into our chains and running suits.

On February 16, 1987, Tracy and I were taken to another location and were put into chains for the first time. We were manacled either at the wrist or the ankle. The chain was then fixed to a radiator and secured by what looked to me like a simple Yale lock. The chain was only about two or three feet long and didn't allow us much freedom of movement, but worst of all, the chains would remain on us for the rest of our captivity.

It was here that we were placed with a French hostage. This man was to have a profound effect on all the remaining years I spent in captivity. His name was Jean-Louis Normandin. He was a slightly built, handsome young fellow, who worked for a television station in Paris. They had been filming in Beirut eleven months before, when he and his entire crew were abducted. That was shortly after two terrorists were arrested in Paris and put into a French prison.

The crew had been sent to Beirut to cover Terry Waite's appeal for the release of all hostages. Waite was in Beirut to meet with the leaders of the Hezbollah movement, who were holding the hostages. Jean-Louis Normandin's television crew had been in the country only one day, and after covering Terry Waite's meeting with Sheik Fadlallah, were taken hostage themselves.

The crew was released several months after their abduction—but they held on to Jean-Louis Normandin.

He was sitting on the floor of the room we were taken to, chained to the radiator, blandly reading a book. I think he was as surprised to see us as we were to see him. We were chained beside him, and Tracy began his muttering again. Jean-Louis looked at me questioningly, and I slowly tapped the side of my head with one finger, out of Edward's sight. Normandin rolled his eyes, and then looked at me with great sympathy. I think he was trying to convey that he had some idea of what it would be like to be chained to a man who was in such deep mental distress.

While I was instantly impressed with this calm, self-assured Frenchman, Edward felt otherwise. For some reason he took an immediate dislike to Jean, and during his more lucid moments he bluntly told him so. Fortunately, or unfortunately for Tracy, that wasn't often. Jean was always a diplomat and treated Edward as he might a recalcitrant child. I was in the middle and tried to mediate a more peaceful relationship between the two, but it was always touch and go.

I asked Jean what he was reading and he held up the cover. With my blurred vision, I had to squint to read the title.

"Baudelaire. A book of poems," he said.

His English was very halting and my French was no better, but somehow we were able to communicate. As the months went by we became much more skillful at speaking with each other. I noticed that another book lying beside him was *A Beginner's Introduction to English.*

"I wish I had some books to read," I told him.

"You have none?" I shook my head.

"I arrange it for you," he said calmly. I was amazed at how confidently he said this and wondered what mysterious influence he had over our captors. I would learn that Jean had developed an inner strength and assuredness that created a kind of aura around him. Even the guards seemed to respond to it.

I told him that it wouldn't do much good, since my glasses had been smashed when I was abducted in '86 and had never been replaced.

"I fix that, too," he said, with the same air of certainty. He shook his head sadly. "So long with no reading. It must drive you mad." And then he looked furtively at Edward, who was still muttering, lost in the prison of his mind.

Jean was as good as his word. Soon, a guard brought me a paper bag filled with eyeglasses and told me to find a suitable pair. I rummaged through them excitedly, like a child at Christmastime. I tried pair after pair, but none of them seemed to work. Then I hit upon the idea of placing two of them together, and then I could see well enough to read. My pleasure was somewhat tempered, though, when I recognized one of them as having belonged to my friend Peter Kilburn, the AUB librarian who had been murdered and whose body I had identified in the hospital morgue.

Then books were brought to me. Most of them were wildly unsuited to my taste, but I devoured every one. I read *Everything You Wanted to Know About Sex But Were Afraid to Ask!* I memorized *Jane Eyre* and *Robin Hood* almost in their entirety. I read the Koran over a hundred times, and *A Brief History of Time.* I hungrily reentered a world I thought I had lost. Through Normandin's influence, my captors had allowed the most important part of my being—my mind—to escape.

In gratitude, I wanted to share my hoard of books with Normandin, and began to teach him the English language. He was very quick, very facile, and it wasn't long before we were able to chat comfortably together. We had an Arabic dictionary and, like eager schoolchildren, we tackled that language. It helped to make the hours fly much more quickly.

But Normandin had a far greater lesson to teach me: the art of survival. When we were first put together, he had noticed my desperate war against deterioration, and from his own bitter experience, he gave me new ways to fight it.

Jean warned me, above all, never to raise my hopes when I was promised freedom. "Don't expect to be free until it actually happens," he said. It was a special torture, he said, to allow a hostage to dress and prepare for release, and then withhold it. He knew. It had happened to him many times. I remembered the time when I had been promised release and the crushing despair I had felt when it was withdrawn. I vowed never to let that happen again. In the coming years

I would be promised freedom fifteen or twenty times, but I had made the decision never to expect to be let go, even on the day that I was actually let go.

I now had a new weapon to fight despair.

Jean also said never to offend the guards in any way; it was the fastest way to get killed. I remember how enraged the guards had been when Tracy's rantings had offended them. He had been beaten half to death. On another occasion he had written the guards a note saying he was Jewish, hoping, I suppose, that they would execute him. Again, he had been severely beaten. Then there was the time on the balcony when angry guards made us face the wall and told us we would be shot. For a fleeting moment they may have come close to carrying out the threat. Outward passiveness and inner iron were the ways to survive captivity.

It was also critical, Jean said, to stay active, both physically and mentally. No matter how constricted our confinement, we had to try to work out every day. We had to reach deep inside ourselves to find the inner strength we knew was there. I accepted Jean's advice wholeheartedly and found that not only were my mind and body greatly improved, but the regimen imposed a structure on the days that made the endless weeks and months of captivity much easier to bear.

Even as I drained away as a person, I found myself growing as a soul. I found myself preparing my life for when I became a free man again. And I was building an absolute assuredness that one day I would be set free. I had come to realize that the only way to fight hopelessness and despair was to keep busy, to search my mind and body for the strength and spirit that I had found was there. It exists in every person, I think. But to discover it demands a private journey, a personal adventure that no one can take for us.

I will always be grateful to Jean for pointing me in the right direction.

To my further astonishment, I discovered that our guards' treatment of us improved remarkably from almost the first moment we were put together with Normandin. I could never quite understand the strange, charismatic effect he had over them. Suddenly we became a part of their daily ritual and routine.

Tracy and I were accustomed to being fed only once a day, on rare occasions twice. Now we were placed on a fixed and more generous program.

We were fed three times a day, much better food that often included fresh fruit and vegetables. We were allowed more bathroom privileges, including more frequent baths and showers, and, oh, how wonderful that was! We were also given a change of clothing every few weeks, usually military fatigues, but freshly washed. I began to feel like a new man again.

I also learned a great deal more about the men who were guarding us. They were mostly young people who were trying to exist in the war-torn country of Lebanon, where the unemployment rate reached 45 percent. Working as captors was the only employment they could find.

Some who had lost friends and loved ones in the war were intensely bitter. They were volatile and liable to administer unprovoked beatings without mercy. These I learned to keep at a respectable distance.

One guard particularly stands out in my mind. He had been away from his hilltop home in Lebanon one day and returned to discover that his entire family had been blown to bits in a shelling attack. An Israeli tank had driven up to it and fired at point-blank range, because of a suspicion that the house was holding terrorists.

I expressed my sorrow and quietly asked if he held any deep hatred in his heart. No, he said, the Koran spoke against bitterness. It taught forgiveness. He accepted the loss of his family as the will of Allah.

Though we barely spoke each other's language, I learned

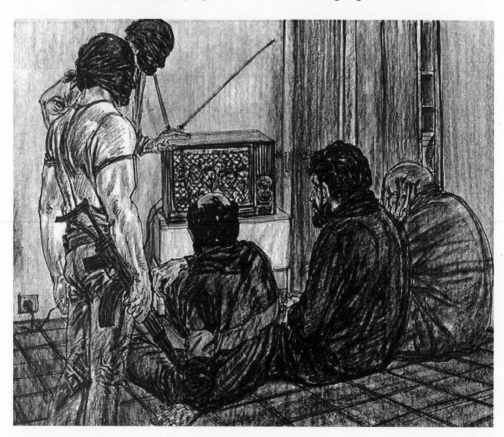

from this one small star in a dark sky that hatred has a weight as tangible as a rock; that the more hate I carried, the more I would be dragged down and left exhausted. That understanding helped to teach me that the energy we spend in gathering bitterness is only self-destructive—that I was more whole, more spiritually alive, when I let it go. Forgiveness is the basis of the philosophy that I think helped me to survive.

In the months that followed, Normandin and I spent almost all our waking hours together. Although we continued to feel great pity for Edward Tracy, the intensity of our conversations, our daily language lessons, and our exchanges of books and ideas almost shut out his constant moanings and mutterings.

Normandin and I had become more like brothers than friends. I made him promise that if he was the first to be released he would contact my wife, Elham, and let her know that I was all right. She was constantly on my mind, and I may have spoken about her to the point of tedium. But Jean always sat patiently, a half-smile on his lips, and listened. He understood that the pain of separation and loneliness was worse than any cruelty the guards could inflict on us.

The day came in November 1987 when the guards came in and told us that Tracy and I were about to be released. We were given a fresh change of clothing and told to prepare ourselves. I was about to ask about Normandin, but then thought better of it. I remembered what Jean had repeatedly said: "Never trust anything your captors tell you."

He was right again. Shortly after, they told us that we were not going home—that Jean-Louis was the man to be released.

This time I was prepared for just such a cruel hoax and did not feel a maddening disappointment. And, although I would greatly miss his company and his strong inspiration, I was happy that my friend would be free after his twenty months of captivity.

I can't deny there were times when I felt lost, abandoned by my own people, my own government. I would sometimes think that nobody cared what happened to us. In fact, after I was released, my brother Tom showed me a television interview program from Florida in which a woman caller said that hostages had had plenty of warnings, that we were selfish, and were getting just what we deserved. So I was not altogether wrong.

But we were told nothing except for occasional scraps of misinformation. For example, once I was told by a guard that President Reagan had been assassinated in New York and that the American government was in chaos. Knowing our elective system, I knew that the chaos part couldn't possibly be true. But for a long time I did believe the president was dead.

After two, three, four years, I did begin to wonder what was happening. Why couldn't the most powerful nation in the world get us released?

Long years later I learned that the British and American governments were apparently incapable of solving the hostage problem. Colonel Oliver North was trying to swap TOW missiles with Iran for American hostages, only to see the Ayatollah renege on his promises. This, of course, resulted in the infamous Iran-Contra episode. Terry Waite had some early success in freeing some British men, but then was taken hostage himself.

The French seemed to be the most successful in freeing their hostages. Though they had agreed with Washington's policy of not dealing with the terrorists, they simply bent the rules a bit.

Jacques Chirac, the French prime minister, entrusted the business of dealing with the various underground groups in the Middle East to Jean-Charles Marchiana, who had close ties to Lebanese Shia. Those ties enabled him to deal directly with the Hezbollah, and, by making various concessions, he was able to obtain the release of both Jean-Louis and Roger Anque, one of the few French journalists in West Beirut at the time he was abducted by the Islamic Jihad. I will never understand why my country couldn't have used some skillful, back-door diplomacy to get the Americans released. If there is any bitterness left in me, it is because of those strict non-negotiation policies and the intractable views of the British and Israeli governments. But I hold no hatred for any individual involved in those terrible days, including the guards and the people who had taken me. A spirited French filmmaker and a saddened but forgiving Lebanese guard had taught me well.

Eventually, I learned that Roger Anque and Normandin returned to hero receptions in Paris. I can imagine Normandin's modest reaction to such a celebration: a small Gallic shrug of his shoulders, a slight smile on his lips. He had learned how to endure anything, even accolades and momentary fame. And I discovered that he was true to his word. Soon after his release, he telephoned Elham in Beirut.

Chapter 4

Elham: I had been everywhere, tried everything, but still I had had no news of Joseph, even whether or not he was alive. I was deeply concerned because the warring parties in the Middle East seemed to grow more intense every day.

There were so many underground groups you could hardly count them. The PLO had been the most popular, the most supported, and the best known until they were banished from the country after the Israeli invasion of Lebanon in 1982. But their leader, Yasir Arafat, had become an international figure.

Then there were the Nasserists who were well established in the Sunni community and who believed in a pan-Arabist ideology; the Lebanese National Movement, founded by Kamal Joumblatt; the Amal, founded by Nabih Birri; the Lebanese forces (Phalangists); and the Hezbollah, or the "Party of God." The list goes on and on.

I was willing to approach any of them in order to reach the Revolutionary Justice Organization, the RJO, which I knew was holding my husband. But I was never successful.

Then, one night, I received a phone call from a man whose voice I did not recognize. He said his name was Jean-Louis Normandin and that he was calling me from the French Embassy in Beirut.

Jean-Louis told me that he had been a fellow hostage with Joseph for nine months, that he and my husband had become fast friends, and that he had promised to call me if he were the first to be released.

It was the first news I had had of how Joseph was doing. I was thrilled and asked if I could meet Jean in Paris. I would take the earliest flight from Beirut. He said, of course; he would meet me at the airport.

I don't remember where we had lunch or what I had to eat, I was so anxious to hear news about Joe. Nothing he told me was reassuring. It was quickly apparent that he was not going to fill me with false hopes.

In a very soft voice, he told me that the life of a hostage was difficult and demanded a great deal of courage and inner strength, but that Joseph had proven over and over again that he possessed those qualities. It came as no surprise to me.

He told me of Edward Tracy, for whom I felt instant pity, but sadness as well, that Joseph had that extra burden to bear. He told me of the guards and the conditions in which the hostages lived, and, while his descriptions didn't fill me with joy, I knew with certainty that Joseph would endure it all and that I would see him again. That was my prayer. That was my belief. And my faith would help me to endure many crises in the years to come.

When I left Normandin, I flew to the United States to give the family the latest news. It was a hard trip, meeting them without Joseph for the first time. I tried to reassure them, but we were all pained by the knowledge of what Joseph was going through. I told them what Normandin said to me: that Joseph was bearing up well and that, together, he and Jean-Louis had built a private inner fortress of strength and spirit that no one could penetrate.

Now I was more determined than ever to find some way to get Joe released. And I was not alone in my resolve. Everywhere in the West and Middle East, families of hostages were doing everything they could to bring their loved ones home to them.

The mother of British hostage John McCarthy was suffering from terminal cancer and had only a few months to live. She made a direct appeal to his captors in a television broadcast, saying, "Please, let him go. Let me see him one more time before I die."

There was no response, and so the family made a similar appeal. Mrs. McCarthy had only a few more days to live, they said. Would her son's captors please help them? She died without seeing her son or even knowing whether he was still alive. The kidnappers let her die with her prayers left unanswered. Some years later, I would find myself making a similar appeal on Lebanese television. But in America, Joseph's family in Pennsylvania rallied their support in an effort to obtain his freedom. His brother, Thomas, and his sons, Joseph, Jr., and David, buttonholed every congressman they could get to. They knocked on every door and found, as I had in Lebanon, that not every door would open to them. They appeared on countless television news and interview programs, trying to let the world know of the injustice being done to Joseph and begging the support of anyone who could help us.

This is a very quiet and peaceful family. But now they fought like tigers, and they never let up, day or night, for the five long years that Joseph was a captive.

Thomas, normally a very retiring, almost shy man, even erected a huge display on the lawn in front of his house. It showed the names of all the hostages and the number of days that each had been held. Of course, it attracted worldwide attention and teams of reporters and cameramen came to his home to interview him. He didn't turn away a single one. The display was a brilliant idea to interest the media, which was what Thomas had planned all along. He wanted the world never to forget the plight of his brother, never to think that Joseph was yesterday's news. And he was hopeful that a news report might somehow reach a person in a position to help.

Joseph's sisters, Helen and Rose, had both been diagnosed with cancer. Like Sheila McCarthy, they both desperately wanted to survive until they could see their loved one again.

I was so inspired by the family's love and devotion. They were Joseph's voice in America, and I was his in Lebanon. We were determined to knock on every door, to badger the same people, and to try endlessly to reach the RJO, the group that was holding my husband.

It may have seemed hopeless, but I never gave up hope. Joseph's family proved to me that I wasn't alone in my struggle, and letters poured in from sympathetic people all over the world. In some ways, I was a captive like my husband. I didn't have to endure his suffering—which I would have willingly shared if I could have only been with him—but my grief was like a heavy stone in my heart that I had to carry with me every day for all those years.

Chapter 5

Joseph: After Normandin left, I sometimes tried to imagine what he was doing at that very moment. Probably sitting in a quiet Parisian cafe, sipping a small brandy, surrounded by admirers listening raptly to every word he had to say about his life as a hostage. I wondered if he would mention me, and the language lessons and the inspired conversations we had shared. Then, of course, I knew he would. We had become brothers in captivity, and he had helped to nurture me through some of the worst moments in my captivity. I knew in my heart that he would be true to his promise. He would call Elham soon after his release and let her know that I was all right.

Elham was constantly on my mind. I remembered our wedding and how joyfully we had danced together. I had her picture in my mind—her dark, lustrous eyes, her soft smile. I thought how fortunate I was to have known her, even for such a short time. We had been married little more than a year before I was abducted.

After so many months in a series of bleak prison chambers, I had built up torturous yearnings. How I wanted to see the clear, blue sky again, the warming sun, the blaze of stars in the night heaven. But more than anything, I wanted desperately to recover the lost love and comfort of my wife and family.

My separation from humanity was worse than any beating my captors could inflict on me. Worse—almost—than death.

I began to fix the images of my loved ones in my mind. I began to assign each mental image a fixed place on the wall of every prison where we were being held and to call them to mind at a glance. Through my imagination, I found a way of decorating those barren cells.

After Normandin's release, the attitude of most of the guards seemed to cool toward Tracy and me. Edward's mental state seemed to worsen by the day. He would lie on his pallet, shut out from the world, often moaning, muttering, sometimes weeping. I think this was as unnerving to the guards as it was to me. And yet I felt great sorrow for Tracy. He was as powerless to change his condition as I was to be rid of him, which I frankly admit I wished for. I couldn't understand why our captors simply didn't release him, a poor, tortured man unable to even understand the reasons for his painful captivity. But I don't blame Tracy for the guards' change in behavior. It was probably that I simply lacked the mystique that seemed to come so naturally to Jean-Louis. The guards didn't start to abuse us physically, they just appeared to be more distant, and some of the privileges we had enjoyed while Normandin was with us were slowly withdrawn.

Yet, I had been left an extraordinary legacy. I was now able to deal with my captivity in a way that I hadn't imagined earlier. While chained, I was now exercising daily. Even though the space in which I was able to move was never more than about four square feet, I would do push-ups, sit-ups, stretching exercises, whatever came to mind. And when I finished with this regimen, I would always feel physically stronger. During the rest of my confinement, I rarely skipped a workout.

I tried to keep my mind active as well. Each day I would sit, meditatively, and attempt to reach inside myself to find the wellsprings of strength and spirit that were so essential to my survival. They were there, I was sure of it. Normandin had convinced me that there was a stronger man within me than I had ever imagined.

And I still had my precious books. I think there is almost no greater anguish than being deprived of books, of being able to transport ourselves into other times, of the thoughts of other men and women, of a vision of the world around us. I agonized with Jane Eyre, romped through the forests of Sherwood with Robin Hood and his Merry Men, got great spiritual solace and understanding from the Koran. But I must confess that if they had offered me some such book as *Nancy Drew and the Girl Detectives*, I would eagerly have accepted it. In many ways, reading was my redemption. It permitted me to escape for long periods of time during the years of my confinement. Had some of my captors known that, I think they might have smashed my makeshift eyeglasses to the ground. Without realizing it, they had given me a measure of freedom.

As a hostage, my most despairing moments came at Christmastime. Our large family in Norristown, Pennsylvania, had always celebrated the holiday with joy and love. Affection for each other would pour out of us in a loving way that we weren't always able to express during the rest of the year.

I was thinking of those past Christmases on December 24, 1987, when the guards burst into our room at about 7:30 that night and told us to prepare. We were about to be moved.

Almost every time we were taken from one location to another, the warning would be as abrupt and unexpected as that. Once again we were trussed and blindfolded and crammed into the trunk of a car. I had learned how to be as compliant as possible, which made the guards' handling of me a little gentler. Edward, though, who never understood what was happening to him, might have been treated a bit more roughly. I think the guards understood that they were dealing with a seriously ill man, but they never seemed to learn how to handle him. I think if they had spoken softly to him, given him an encouraging pat on the back now and then, he would have been much more tractable. But that isn't the way they treated hostages.

We were taken only a short distance away.

The room was as barren as the others.

Here we would spend Christmas Eve, 1987.

There was only a single bulb in the room, hanging from the ceiling, but either it had been turned off or the bulb was dead. I lay there in the darkness thinking about Elham and what she was doing at that moment. I imagined us sitting together next to our Christmas tree having an intimate dinner. I saw the faces of my relatives and friends, and wondered how they were enjoying the holiday season. My children, my brothers and sisters—all their images were clear in my mind. Silently I wished them a merry, merry Christmas.

I was, as you might imagine, in despair. But then I began to remember Normandin's admonition to never allow myself to sink into a mire of self-pity. "You might never emerge again," he had said.

And so I began trying to strengthen my inner self again. In *Moby Dick*, Ishmael says, "What if some great hunk of a sea captain orders me to sweep down the deck? What does that indignity amount to, weighed, I mean, in terms of the New Testament?" Recalling that, I resolved to reinforce my sense of humility, my feelings of forgiveness, my determination to survive, and to become a better man than I had ever been.

Almost at that moment a guard came in carrying a single lighted candle. Silently, he handed it to me and then left the room.

The light it cast over the walls had almost mystical proportions. It was as though it contained all the warmth, hope, and life that was left inside me. In every way it was, to me, truly symbolic of the season. That small gift, brought to me by a hooded guard in the darkness of a Christmas night, renewed my spirit. I nurtured every flickering spark as though it were my last breath. When it finally sputtered out, I was able to lie back on my pallet and sleep sweetly. For the first time in my life, I felt that I had discovered the true meaning of Christmas: that the smallest gifts are the greatest; that God exists within all of us—every Christian, every Muslim, every Jew, and that we need only to seek him out for ourselves. I was also calmed by the Islamic concept of *kismet*, that our fate has been decided long ago and can only be denied by the resolve of our own inner spirit.

We were kept at the "Christmas site" until May of 1988, when we were moved to yet another location. It was near the airport; all night long I could hear the sounds of planes landing and taking off, and the roaring sound of a large searchlight scanning the sky above us.

The nine days previous to the move had been filled with the sounds of heavy bombardments. At times they became a crescendo of artillery and mortar explosions mixed with small-arms fire, which made me feel as though the world was coming to an end—that Beirut was slowly melting into a fiery cauldron that would suddenly erupt and blow us all into oblivion.

I have only the greatest respect for those men who served in Vietnam, especially the soldiers and airmen who were taken hostage. But they had been trained for such a situation. Those held at prison camps like the Hanoi Hilton had others around them to help them through their ordeal.

As an American businessman caught up in a war that I had no real part in, I was a little bit different. I didn't have the background, the training, to carry me through what often seemed to be endless captivity. I had to learn to find my own way through those terrible five years.

But thanks, in large part, to Jean-Louis, I had prepared myself to confront whatever fate had in store for me. I remember the young Arab guard who had lost his entire

family and said, "It was the will of Allah." I thought his sad
acceptance spoke of a wisdom far beyond his years. There
are some things over which we have no control. We can
only try to fortify ourselves in order to meet, as strongly as
possible, whatever crisis comes to pass.

The constant shelling had probably made our captors as
jittery as we were. That might have been the reason we were
so abruptly and unexpectedly shifted to the airport site.
Here, I imagine, our safety was considered more secure. The
house was located close to the end of a runway for landing
aircraft. We could hear the planes cutting down their engines
as they descended to the runway and, much more distantly
now, the sounds of heavy gunfire. I suspect the airport was
off limits to any artillery attack; it was, after all, as valuable
to the Islamic Jihad as it was to anyone who had to move in
and out of Beirut—though over the years the airport had to
be closed many times due to shelling.

Our new cell was a small, barren room about four by
eight feet. It contained only a bookcase at one end and two
sleeping pallets that covered most of the floor space. I
continued to act almost deferentially toward the guards and,
on occasion, we would have small conversations, "Are you
married?" "What's your wife's name?" That sort of thing.
But it wasn't too often. The guards were almost invariably
young, blue-collar, Lebanese working men. They thought of
their duties as a job, something they desperately needed to
help feed their families. Ninety percent of the time, they
did only what they had to do and left the room. The few
who did talk to us just said what they wanted to say, good
or bad.

My friend David Jacobsen, who had been kidnapped more
than a year before I was, told me later that he had asked
other hostages how I was doing. They told him fine, that I
got along unfailingly well with the guards. But how they
could have known that, I can't say. The only other hostages
I was ever with were Tracy and Normandin. I had been held
briefly with four other men who were in an adjoining room,
but I never saw their faces nor was I allowed to speak to
them.

Tracy continued to have occasional trouble with the

guards. His constant mutterings and ranting seemed to unnerve them. They had, in fact, not realized his disturbed condition until three months after we were thrown together. By that time he was a mass of bruises—not surprisingly, since he was often beaten with a heavy length of telephone cable.

There were times when such loneliness and deep sorrow crept through my defenses that I almost envied Tracy. I would look at him lying on his pallet, muttering some strange gibberish, and think how his mind had taken him far from the brutality of his confinement. I prayed that wherever he was gave him some moments of peace and serenity. I would come to realize, though, how much more fortunate I was than my tragic friend. My mind was intact, my soul and spirit growing stronger every day. I had hope. He had none. Edward was a captive twice over.

Three months before we were moved to the airport location, Marine Lt. Col. William Higgins was kidnapped. I would never meet him, but our lives would one day become

closely and tragically involved.

Higgins was abducted while working with a United Nations Peacekeeping Mission in southern Lebanon. The man who allegedly ordered the kidnapping was Sheikh Abdul Karim Obeid, a well-known Lebanese Shia cleric with intimate ties to the Hezbollah. Obeid was also suspected of masterminding the abduction of two Israeli soldiers who had been taken while on patrol in southern Lebanon in 1986. All our lives would become inextricably involved in a tragic drama to be played out little more than a year later.

But at this time, in May of 1988, I felt as secure as I was ever to feel while a captive. I continued to plumb my mind to find the powerful energy I knew existed there. I kept myself as active as possible while chained to a radiator or hooked to a rusty sink, doing exercises, walking endlessly around the confining space that my captors had allowed me. Three steps this way, two steps that, sharp right turn and head for home. I often played silly, almost childish, games, but they helped to keep me alert and alive. Also, I had the luxury of my books and devoured them endlessly. I don't think any young reader ever got more excitement and pleasure from the adventures of Robin Hood than I did. Or felt more sympathy for the sad fortunes of Jane Eyre. These books were alive for me and took me to worlds far distant from the confines of my imprisonment.

After the beatings, tortures, and threats of execution, I began to feel that my captors could do nothing worse to me.

Even some of the terrorists' cruelest tricks may have backfired on them. Many times they brought me writing materials and told me I could contact my loved ones or anyone on the outside. "Tell them how you are feeling, how we are treating you. Anything you like. We won't read the letters," they said. Of course, I knew they would. If I ever suggested that I was being mistreated in any way, I think the sky would have fallen in on me. I was allowed only four official letter-writing sessions. I wrote three to Elham, as full of as much love and hope as I was able to express. I never failed to mention how humanely I was being treated and how kind and generous my captors were. The fourth letter, which I was ordered to write, was to President Reagan, pleading with him to change American policy toward the Middle East, to find a peaceful solution to the hostage situation, and to bring us all home again.

I prayed that those letters would actually be delivered, but it was too much to hope for. One day my suspicions were confirmed when I found torn shreds of letters I had written. They had been ripped up and thrown into the toilet. Still, whenever I had a chance to get pencil and paper, I wrote letters to Elham, all of my family in America, and to close friends in the United States and Beirut. By now I knew that they wouldn't be sent, but I wrote them anyway. It was another form of therapy.

I think the terrorists' motives for those writing exercises were twofold. First, they wanted to know the state of my mind, the feelings I might have about my captors, and how vulnerable I had become after months and years as a hostage. Secondly, I believe they wanted to see if they could catch a cryptic message that I might include in any of the letters in order to reach an outside agent. Of course, there were none. But their paranoia made them think that any and every American in Beirut was a spy. The slightest error, even the most inadvertent, would confirm their suspicions that I was CIA. Once they were convinced of that, however unfairly, I don't believe I would have lived very long.

It may sound fanciful, this notion that you could be beaten or even condemned for even the most innocent infraction, but it was the truth of all the hostages' daily existence.

Not long after the death of the CIA Chief, William Buckley, who had died in captivity, David Jacobsen was ordered to make a video statement prepared by the Islamic Jihad. In it, he was told to say that Buckley had been "executed" because of Washington's unwillingness to deal with the hostage-takers.

David knew otherwise. He had listened to Buckley's last agonized days, heard him crying out before he died for pancakes with blueberry syrup. The probability is that if the government had acted quickly, Buckley might have been spared. The CIA director had been badly beaten and tortured by his captors, but they might have saved him if they had wished to.

Instead, they used Buckley, who was no longer important to them, as a threat to the Western nations. This was what might happen to all of the hostages, they wanted to suggest, unless the West was willing to negotiate.

Jacobsen dutifully read the prepared statement, as anyone would in the circumstances, anyone who placed some value on their life. But when he got to the passage where he was to announce that Buckley had been "executed" because of Washington's intransigence, he became emotionally overwhelmed. He ad libbed an expression of sympathy to Buckley's wife and children. But Buckley had no wife. No child. And the Hezbollah thought that David had tried to transmit a coded message to the Central Intelligence Agency, which was truly preposterous. Nonetheless, about a week later, David was mercilessly interrogated, severely beaten, and left in solitude with every bone and muscle in his body aching.

Fortunately, they found nothing suspicious in my correspondence, and even though I had discovered the torn leaves of many letters in the bathroom, I continued to write them whenever they allowed me to.

I don't think they realized that they had given me another tool to fight off the sometimes overwhelming feelings of loneliness and abandonment.

Despite knowing that they would probably never be delivered, I continued to write letters. Always to Elham. Endlessly to my sons, my brothers and sisters, my family and friends in Lebanon and America. I sometimes felt as though they could hear my sentiments, even though they would never read the thoughts and emotions that poured out of me. Those "dead" letters gave me the opportunity to express the love I had for my wife, my family, and my close friends, and to help reassure me that I was still part of the world outside.

Had the terrorists known how the simple exercise of writing a letter had so emboldened and strengthened me, they might not have offered me such a wonderful gift. A stub-nosed pencil, a few sheets of lined paper, and I was able to give expression to the thoughts and feelings I had kept repressed inside me for so long.

On June 19, 1988, the guards once again burst into our room. "Up!" they said. "Cicippio, Tracy, you are going to another place."

Another place could mean anything, and so each move was a kind of perilous adventure in itself. They might be taking us to the same remote beach where my friend Peter Kilburn had been murdered. We might even be freed, but I never dared to think about that.

Tracy and I were blindfolded as usual, led to an

automobile, and put in the trunk. I had learned the routine by now, and lay down as compliantly and silently as possible, with my knees curled up and my head seeking a softer place to rest. Then I drifted into meditation, into a silent world where I could think of Elham and the wonderful moments we had spent together. Of my family. Of the world outside. I tried to resist any negative thoughts of what fate had in store for me. Whatever happened, would happen. The Islamic concept of *kismet* was strong in my mind and gave me certitude and peace.

I was shaken out of my thoughts when the car's engine stopped. The trunk was wrenched open and a voice demanded, "Out! Now!" I went willingly, happy to enjoy a few precious moments of the open air, breathing it deeply into my lungs before we were thrust into the trunk of a second car.

The exchange, from one auto to another, happened four times on this long and arduous trip. I would always remember to draw in as much as I could of the sweet, fresh air of freedom. I could feel the warmth of the sun, breathe in the rich fragrance of the foliage around us, before I was again thrown into the trunk of another car. My captives were so confident that at times they would pull into a service station and fill up with gas while I was lying in the trunk. They knew what I knew; if I cried out for help, I was a dead man.

There was no way of knowing where we were being driven, but any long trip gave me the assurance that we weren't going to be shot. It wasn't a long distance to the killing grounds, and this ride, being taken from one car and stuffed into the trunk of another, seemed to take an eternity.

It was a little more than an hour later that we arrived at our new location. I was concerned, as always in these interminable shifts, with whether the new guards would treat us as ruthlessly as some had in the past. Would I be beaten, tortured, endlessly threatened with losing my life once again? And how would they react to the strange behavior of my friend Edward Tracy? I hoped that they would be more kindly to him, understand that he was a grievously sick man, and treat him gently.

As it turned out, the room we were taken to at this new site was probably the nicest of all the places in which we were kept confined. It even had some furnishings. As well as the makeshift beds we were usually allowed, there was a huge, mirrorless chiffonier in one corner. Huge box mattresses had been placed against the window, blocking any view we might have of the outside, but even that seemed less oppressive than the boarded-up windows we had become accustomed to. Most astonishing of all was a wall-to-wall carpet that covered the floor. It wasn't exactly the Ritz-Carlton, but this new place gave us a small measure of home-like comfort, of which we had been deprived for so long.

The area around the house was very quiet. We hardly ever heard the sound of traffic or of people passing by, and so that added an amount of quietude and repose. Even the guards, if not overly kind to us, were civil. They went silently about their duties, led us to the bathroom when we asked them to, and fed us reasonably well, though not extravagantly. At times we were even given some fresh fruit, like grapes, which always came as a special treat. They said little more than hello, but that, too was a small blessing. I thought about trying to engage them in conversation once or twice, but came to realize that it might be a futile, even dangerous, effort.

I knew we were outside the city of Beirut, and suspected we were in Sidon, on the outskirts of the city. After the Israeli invasion of Lebanon, Sidon became a hotbed of Palestinian terrorism, even in the refugee camps that had been set up by the Israeli government. The prisoners, some of whom escaped, were largely supported by Abu Nidal, who headed one of the most feared groups of Palestinian terrorists in the Middle East. It was Abu Nidal who had ordered the murder of Kenneth Whitty, a British embassy secretary in Athens, who had been shot dead on his way home for lunch. It was he who had demanded the execution of Alec Collett, an elderly British journalist, in retaliation for Britain's refusal to release two Arabs held in a British prison after an attempt to assassinate the Israeli ambassador there. Collett was forced to make a video statement directly appealing to the British prime minister, Margaret Thatcher, to release the Arab prisoners or he would be executed. She turned a deaf ear. Washington's mandate of no dealing for hostages was all she would listen to. Shortly after, another videotape was released showing Alec Collett hanging from a makeshift gallows. Mrs. Thatcher sent her "heartfelt sympathy" to the grieving family.

Our guards' behavior toward us might change overnight, at times almost from moment to moment. I began to feel that these sudden mood shifts were triggered by events on the outside.

For example, in July 1989, the destroyer *USS Vincennes* mistakenly shot down an Iranian airbus with an enormous loss of life. Our guards were surely aware of this event, and at such times a noticeable coolness would set in. At least, that's my guess. Any outside news, even about events that were disparaging of the United States, continued to be withheld from us. The only news we were given was misinformation, obviously designed to lower our spirits, like the false description of President Reagan's death in New York. I must admit I did believe that one for some time, though. I didn't think the guard who told it to me had the imagination to invent such a wild story.

But Normandin's advice stayed with me and served me well for the last four years of my captivity. "If a guard tells you the sun is shining, expect there's a tropical storm raging outside," he had said. Of course, that was especially true if they told us we were about to be repatriated. I never fell for that one again, not even when I was all dressed up in a fresh change of clothing. I might have hoped, at times, but I never allowed myself the momentary luxury of actually believing it, and so I never had to experience that crushing disappointment.

I don't think the false freedom stories were just a cruel joke that our captors were playing on us. I think they were a carefully thought-out psychological ploy to keep us subdued. The more depressed we were, the easier we were to control. I don't know of a single other hostage kept in captivity for any length of time who wasn't promised freedom only to have it withdrawn.

We were only held at the "June site" for about four months. On October 12, 1988, we were moved by car in the usual manner to a new location about five minutes away. It was there that some of my worst fears were realized.

The house was in another quiet area, but beyond that it bore little resemblance to our former site. The guards included some very bitter men who had lost family members and friends in the fighting. Naturally, they took their hatred out on us. The smallest incident might provoke a slap, a kick, a punch, even a series of blows raining down on us. And of course, Edward Tracy was an incident by himself.

Like the earlier guards, these men didn't seem to realize that Tracy was a sick man, and when I tried to explain it to them, they told me to shut up and threatened me with the butt end of an AK-47.

We were repeatedly told that we might be executed, although I never really took those threats seriously. For some reason our captors, at least the higher-ups, continued to think we were important hostages. Besides, I had continued to build my inner fortress, figuratively speaking, brick by brick, and I felt that I was becoming virtually impregnable. So many times I have felt profoundly grateful to Normandin for showing me the direction I had to take to achieve this. It was the road to my salvation.

Naturally, I was as cooperative and docile as possible while in the presence of the guards. One small mistake— anything to seriously anger one of the embittered guards—and he might fly into a rage and, without meaning to, beat me to death. I sometimes wondered how Tracy had managed to survive for so long. I felt enormous pity for him. He had no way of controlling the behavior that so often enraged our captors.

Some years later, after I was freed, I heard the story of Brian Keenan, a hostage who often deliberately taunted his guards and showed absolute contempt for them. How he managed to survive the terrible beatings they inflicted on him is beyond me. I don't believe I could have, but then Keenan was more than twenty years younger than me.

Keenan was a teacher from the North of Ireland, an Ulster Protestant, but, oddly sympathetic to the Republican cause. Like Dennis Hill, he had come to Beirut to teach English to Lebanese students anxious to pass the entrance examination at the American University. Had he known of David's tragic fate, he might have had second thoughts.

Brian was taken outside his apartment at 5 a.m. and, though he carried an Irish rather than a British passport, he was made a prisoner anyway. It may be because he was reported to have once climbed a tree while a bit intoxicated and yelled out, "We'll get the IRA to sort you Hezbollah bastards out!" It is no surprise to me that he was abducted.

Once a guard accused him of trying to open a small window in his cell. Keenan heatedly denied it and finally grabbed the guard and started to shake him. The guard left the room, but returned moments later with another guard who was built like a gorilla.

While the large guard held Keenan, the smaller guard beat the Irishman mercilessly with a broom handle. Keenan never cried out.

In December of that year, while still at the "Hate House," I looked forward to another bleak Christmas. It was the only time of the year that I might momentarily let my guard down. And in that house, the guards were not about to offer us any niceties or show us any new kindnesses.

In spite of the adversity, the lessons I learned through those long years were unshakable. I would not let myself sink into a mire of despair and self-pity. I was still discovering the strength of the human spirit, the truly spiritual necessity of keeping my mind and body intact.

In that same month, Pan Am Flight 103 was blown up as it flew over the village of Lockerbie in Scotland and fell in a fiery ball to the earth. A total of 276 people were killed, including all the passengers and crew, and other innocents on the ground.

This was Muammar Quadaffi's Christmas present to the free world. It is believed that the bomb which blew the plane apart had been placed by his agents in retaliation for the 1986 bombing of Libya. Others thought it might be a reaction to the shooting down of the Iranian airbus, but the first theory is the stronger.

Had I known of that event, I might have thought the world had gone completely insane. It surely would have brought even greater sorrow to my already sorrowful Christmas season. In withholding news of tragic events such as that, my captors may have been doing me a greater service than they realized. But I can't even recall any discernible difference in the guards' behavior at the time of the Pan Am plane's destruction.

Still, I yearned for news—any news of what was happening in the outside world. I would hear the sounds of a radio from time to time, but I couldn't make out what was being said. They might have been Arabic radio soap operas, for all I knew. I did hear television broadcasts, though, that were probably beamed from Cairo. They were mostly films from the West. I could sometimes make out the sounds of galloping horses, the sounds of televised gunfire, an Indian war cry, and realize that my captors were undoubtedly watching an American western dubbed into Arabic. The sounds the guards made, their vocal reactions, were much the same as an American family might make sitting in the living room watching a John Wayne movie like *True Grit* or *Rooster Cogburn*. In a strange way, the muffled sounds of those movies were almost reassuring. Even though the dialogue was always in Arabic, I was certain that many of the films were from the United States, and I would fantasize that I was sitting in the comfort and safety of a home in America with Elham or, perhaps, other members of my family, enjoying a relaxed evening in front of the TV.

Though it seemed to be endless, we were held at the "Hate House" for sixteen months to the day. On February 12, 1990, the guards came in and told us to prepare to move once again. I quickly gathered up my few belongings and waited for them to come and blindfold me.

The trip was another long one of at least an hour, and I lay in the trunk of the car wondering again how the new guards were going to treat us. Would they abuse us? Beat us? Take my books? Smash my eyeglasses?

What would our living quarters be like? Would they be as mean and vermin-ridden as some of the places where we had been held? I prayed not. What would the food be like? Better? Worse? What kind of bathroom privileges would be allowed? Would we be allowed a bath or shower now and then, and given an occasional change of fresh clothing? And, of course, I always wondered if we hadn't become too much of a burden to them, if our usefulness to their cause had run out, and if they had decided to put an end to us. Some months later, I would learn that both of those last gloomy thoughts had a degree of truth in them.

But the longer the trip took, the more assured that we were simply being moved to another location. If they had wanted to shoot us, it was only a short distance to any number of killing sites.

When at last I emerged from the trunk, I thought I heard unmistakably rural sounds, including the growl of a tractor working a nearby field. I would hear it again many times during the next one-and-a-half years. The air was crisply cold, but smelled sweet and verdant, and once again I breathed it in as deeply as I could.

Tracy and I were led into the house and confined to a room on the ground floor. It was actually the basement of the house, with two more stories rising above it. We were kept in chains, which came as no surprise to me, and there was limited space for us to move around in. I had become very conscious of how much room I would have to perform my daily exercises. The windows were sealed by concrete blocks, and I wondered how much light I would have to continue my reading. I had become immersed in the Koran and read it faithfully in much the same way that a Benedictine monk might devote himself to the Old and New Testaments. Had I been given a Bible, I would have given it the same rapt attention.

At the new location, the treatment by our captors was as good as we could expect. It was certainly not nearly as bad as it had been in some of our other places of confinement. The food wasn't grand or plentiful, but we were given a broader menu.

There were times when I had remembered my mother putting out a huge serving bowl of some fantastic thing she had prepared, some veal and pasta, some broiled chicken, some meatballs, and telling us to all dig in, to help ourselves. She would stand back, smiling, and watch us eat every scrap of those marvelous dinners. By the time we were finished, the bowl was almost as clean as if it had been washed. Of course, there were nine of us children, and we all had healthy appetites.

Remembering those modest but grand moments of my childhood helped to sustain me. I had been raised to understand how wonderful life could be, even in adversity, and I was determined not to surrender that knowledge without a struggle.

Small things, like an unexpected offering of hot coffee, helped to give me encouragement and hope. And the sounds of life outside the farmhouse made me feel that I remained a part of it. Each day I would listen for the early morning sounds of the tractor, and I tried to picture the man who would be perched on the metal seat, devotedly tilling his land. At around five o'clock every afternoon, I anticipated the excited cries and chatter of children emerging from what had to be a school bus. I would listen to the children's voices fading as they wandered from the bus, and then the roar of the engine as the bus was driven away. It sometimes filled me with a kind of sadness, but it also renewed my belief that people are much the same everywhere in the world. Most especially, the children.

The year I was taken to the place that I have come to think of as the "Farm House" was a momentous one in the Middle East. Salman Rushdie, an Anglo-Indian author, released a book called *The Satanic Verses*, which Ayatollah Khomeini considered so blasphemous that he issued a *fatwa*, an edict that virtually condemned the writer to death. It has remained in effect to this writing, and Rushdie has been in hiding ever since.

The Rushdie situation was the first of a series of events that occurred almost month by month and that changed the whole course of the hostage crisis in the Middle East. The happenings came dangerously close to ending my life but, in a fortuitous way, spared it.

In March, the British cut off diplomatic relations with Iran. This was surely no way to negotiate for the release of British captives, to say nothing about the rest of us. While acknowledging that they had the closest fraternal ties to the Middle East, it was the French who had skillfully arranged for the release of the last three of their countrymen held by the terrorists. They had effectively closed the books on the taking of French hostages, and that had been almost a year earlier.

But now there wouldn't even be a dialogue between the British and the Islamic Jihad or even the Syrians to negotiate the release of the hostages. How angry that would have made me feel had I known even the smallest rumor of it. We were just pawns in an endless contest of international gamesmanship, and we would be the first pieces knocked off the board. I wish some of the players had had to spend just a few days as a hostage. I wonder how they would have negotiated then.

The Russian dialogue was quite different than that of the Western powers. One evening four Russians were taken hostage, with one being seriously injured. The following day the Russians took eight hostages of their own who were closely related to the leaders of the Hezbollah. The Russians castrated one of their hostages and sent a message with him to the leaders of the Hezbollah stating they would kill a hostage each day that Russians were held, and if the Russian hostages were not released, then they would take eight more and continue the process. After this statement, all Russian hostages were released within 24 hours.

As an American, fiercely loyal to my country, I still expected that it would eventually come to my support. I don't believe in the credo, "My country, right or wrong," because I thought it was almost invariably right—morally correct. I still do. But if we hadn't stonewalled in this crisis, if we hadn't gone around the Middle East trying to make undercover deals with ruthless leaders like the Ayatollah, sending him TOW and HAWK missiles, for example, and had simply dealt with the hostage-takers openly and in a diplomatic way, I wonder if the hostage problem couldn't have been resolved a lot sooner. At one time there were as many French captives as Americans. France had proved it could be done. But we and the British refused to follow their lead and stubbornly clung to a "no deal" policy. I just wish they had been willing to bend a little. The fact that they didn't took five precious years from my life.

I don't want to sound bitter, because I'm not. Whatever was going through the minds of the policy makers I can't say, and I'm not sufficiently learned in the art of international diplomacy to suggest what I might have done. But I sometimes wonder why all the bright minds in the pools of government were never able to come up with some kind of solution.

Certainly I can understand the reasoning that if you deal with the terrorists, you only encourage them to commit newer and more brutal crimes. But we had clandestine rapprochements with them, anyway. And all you have to do is pick up a morning newspaper to read that kidnappings, murders, and bombings continue to rage in the Middle East and elsewhere in the world.

While I was held at the "Farm House," other events were taking place that would have a direct effect on my life and would also bring me to the very edge of doom. I was blissfully unaware of what was happening and continued to fill my days with the routine that had become so important to my survival.

Here the guards were reasonably civil. There was no "Rifleman," (a name I had given to one particularly embittered guard at our previous location). The "Rifleman" had taken great delight in trying to make our lives as bitter and unpleasant as possible. He would wake us in the middle of the night, brandish the butt end of his rifle, which he always carried, and fire a series of curses and threats at us.

Once he heard me innocently ask another guard if I might have some tea. That enraged him. He pushed me violently to the floor and, towering above me, his rifle poised to strike, he shouted, "This is no hotel, you know!"

When I learned that he had lost his wife and child in the war, I quietly tried to offer him my sympathy. He only scowled and muttered something under his breath. He was a man filled with irrevocable hatred, as were so many in that torn and blighted country. I wished that I could penetrate the angry wall he had built around himself and point out a way to forgiveness and peace. That way was no easy road to travel but, as I would learn, there were great rewards at the end of the journey.

In June of 1989, Ayatollah Khomeini died from the illnesses that had bedeviled him for many of his last years. I sometimes wonder whether his often strange and violent behavior wasn't the result of his failing health. He had always been an irascible and unyielding Shia Muslim, but once thrust upon the world scene, his actions sometimes appeared to be almost demonic. That is certainly the view that people in the Western world had of him. Many terrorist acts, including the taking of hostages, were directly traceable to him. I suspect he will always be remembered as sitting high up on the throne of a powerful Middle Eastern nation, looking sternly out at a world of which he disapproved.

Once again, I can recall no discernible difference in the behavior of the guards, Islamic or not, at the time of the

Ayatollah's demise. I mourn the death of any man. As the
poet John Donne so beautifully expressed it, "Each man's
death diminishes me." I cannot gloat over the loss of a
single life, whether of villain or enemy. I believe in hope,
reform, and redemption, as taught in the Koran, the Bible,
and virtually every other religious text. It is too easy, and
too self-diminishing, to hate.

A month after Khomeini died, Ali Akbar Rafsanjani was
elected president of Iran. I think those two events—the death
of the aged Ayatollah and Rafsanjani's emergence to power—
may have saved my life.

Although I could not know it at the time, I was being
held captive by the Revolutionary Justice Organization, a
group that had been formed in 1985 because of Rafsanjani's
strong encouragement to begin dealing with the West. The
RJO would have none of it, and formed its own party with
other members of the Islamic Jihad, and the Hezbollah—
the "Party of God." Terrorism was their order of the day and
nothing could discourage them from it. The Ayatollah had
even given them his blessing.

After taking power, Rafsanjani didn't have much time to
make an overture to the West before an event of major
importance took place in Lebanon. What happened in the
following weeks proved crucial to my fate, but in a far more
tragic way, to the fate of another American, Marine Lt. Col.
William Higgins.

By late July, Rafsanjani's plans for reconciliation with the
West were well on the way. The head of the United States
National Security Council felt that the new Iranian president
was a man he could deal with, not nearly so intransigent
and fanatical as the Ayatollah. But then the Israelis blundered
onto the scene.

Without warning, and clearly without the approval of
the United States, they kidnapped Sheikh Abdul Karim Obeid
from his villa in Jibchit, an enclave of the Hezbollah in
southern Lebanon.

It was Obeid, the Israelis maintained, who had ordered
the kidnapping of two young Israeli soldiers in the same
year that I was abducted. Obeid would pay for his crimes,
the Israelis angrily announced. But the poor young men

had undoubtedly been executed by that time, and the Israelis must surely have known this. Jewish men did not live long once they were in the hands of the Hezbollah.

Once again it was revenge for revenge's sake and, as far as the hostages were concerned, a grave error by Israel that put the lives of every one of us in jeopardy. Mine in particular.

Of course, I had no idea of what was happening, but I did notice a marked difference in the behavior of the guards around that time. There were no reprisal beatings or anything like that, but they seemed to look at us sternly from time to time, and I thought I could detect a harshness in their voices that suggested they were distraught and angry about something.

And they *were* angry. Obeid was revered by the Islamic Jihad as a man of God and a devoted adherent to their cause. He had a vast army of followers, many of whom, I believe, would have sacrificed themselves to obtain his freedom. A major international crisis had begun. A ticking time bomb had been activated and, as I would discover, I had been placed right next to it.

Within a few days the terrorists holding Lt. Col. Higgins, a group that called itself the Organization of the Oppressed People of the Earth, announced that he would be executed by 12:00 Greenwich mean time on July 31, unless Obeid was immediately and safely returned to Lebanon. Inexorably, the hours passed while the right-wing Israeli government conferred.

For the first time, the relationship between the United States and Israel was severely strained, stretched almost to the limit. A man's life was at stake, but it seemed to mean nothing to the men seated around the conference table in Jerusalem. An American delegate was asked, "Do you think Israel grabbed the sheikh only to free the Western hostages and leave the Israelis behind?" The Israelis must have known that the soldiers, taken three years before and not heard from since, were no longer alive. If they had been, surely the Hezbollah would have produced them, perhaps even offered them in exchange for Obeid. In that regard, it's obvious they were dealing a dead hand, and so they chose

Colonel Higgins to be the victim of their reprisal. I often think of how desolate he must have felt, as the hours of his scheduled execution approached without any response from the Israeli government. They were bartering the soul of a living man for the bodies of two dead men.

Twenty minutes after the deadline, the Israeli government finally responded in a radio report that demanded the release of the soldiers and all the Western hostages. In exchange, they would release all the Shia prisoners held in Israel. They had to know that it was an impossible demand from the Shia's perspective, even if it meant the continued confinement of their beloved Sheikh Obeid. No one was above the cause of Jihad, the Holy War, and Obeid would have been the first to proclaim it.

Less than an hour later, the terrorists released a videotape

showing Colonel Higgins hanging from what appeared to be a hastily built gallows, his body slowly turning. When I later saw the videotape it filled me with unutterable sadness, and, of course, the realization that I had come very close to an identical fate.

I was very moved when I was shown Higgins's last spoken statement on television, which was taped shortly after his abduction in 1988. In an address obviously prepared by his captors, not all of which is clear to me, he said:

"I am William Higgins. In order to get me released, these demands have to be met. One: The withdrawal of Israeli forces from all occupied territories in Lebanon. Two: The release of all detained... Lebanese and Palestinians... from all other prisons inside the Zionist regime in occupied Palestine. Three: The stopping of U.S. intervention in Lebanon and stop sending delegations to the Vietnese [*sic*] area in order to surround the gains of the Islamic revolution in Palestine."

I watched his poor, tortured countenance as he delivered the lines, and the kind of brutality he had been subjected to was immediately clear to me. For a soldier, especially a Marine, to make such absurd demands had to mean that he had been subjected to the most brutal treatment imaginable. I hold nothing but the greatest esteem and the most profound sorrow for Colonel Higgins. But he was a soldier, and I was a businessman. Soon, it would become my turn to face the world and recite words and statements that had been prepared for me.

It would be the most perilous moment in my life. However, many months of reaching within myself for strength and courage had prepared me for it. If it came to it, I would not allow my captors the satisfaction of thinking they had executed a beaten and whimpering man.

Chapter 6

Elham: On the morning of August 2, and like every morning ever since Joseph had been taken, and before washing my face, I had to turn on the radio to follow the latest news that may have affected Joseph's situation. It was like giving Joseph a morning kiss before I started my day. This day was to become the worst in all of Joseph's captivity.

Before leaving for work at the American Embassy, I heard the announcement by the Organization for the Oppressed People of the Earth that they had executed Colonel Higgins, and my blood ran cold. I wondered, fearfully, what they might do to Joseph or to any of the other hostages. At that time, they weren't holding any CIA or military men, just businessmen and teachers. I wondered who was next to be selected if Sheikh Obeid was not released by the Israelis. And then my worst fears were realized.

Upon arriving at my office, the news media announced that unless Sheikh Obeid was immediately released, the Revolutionary Justice Organization would hang Joseph. I was frantic and terrified.

It is not that I wished it to be one of the other hostages. I would have prayed and mourned for any of them. I just couldn't understand why they had selected Joe to be the next victim. He had worked so tirelessly for the people. His door was always open to the victims of the war and their families, and he often reached into his own pocket to help them in their suffering. But perhaps only his family, his relatives, and close friends, the many people he had selflessly given so much to could possibly understand what a kind and generous man he was.

Why Joseph? was the question that kept running through my mind. Why my dear husband who has never done harm to anyone?

While I was in that state of fear and bewilderment, I

heard the phone ringing and ringing. I picked up the receiver, afraid as always that someone was calling with terrible news. In five years, there was not a time I answered the telephone that I didn't expect to hear some word of Joseph. And each time, I hoped that I would hear his voice telling me that he was free and coming home to me.

It was my father. He had heard the horrible news as well. I felt helpless. What was I to do in the middle of this storm? I was thinking of some solution and praying for some help. I called Ambassador John McCarthy. He was very gentle and helpful. We tried to think of ways to spare Joseph's life. He was as helpless as I was. Finally, I thought of calling for a press conference. I knew the power of the press, radio, and television. And, in any case, I realized it was the only way I could reach the people who had taken Joseph, the Revolutionary Justice Organization, and plead to their hearts and consciences to spare my husband's life.

When I wasn't answering questions from some eager reporter or talking into a microphone suddenly thrust into my face or facing a camera and trying to look as brave as I could, I watched all the television news reports. After Colonel Higgins was executed, I watched and listened as President Bush said at a press conference in Washington:

"...I want to comment on a very disturbing report that we just heard, that Colonel Higgins has, indeed, been executed... this matter is of such concern to me and to all of you and the American people, that I think it appropriate that I go back to Washington." [He had been planning a political barnstorming trip in the western United States. He went on to say:] "Whether the report is true or not, for all here, when I try to express my feelings, I know that I speak for the American people... the sense of outrage we all feel about this kind of uncalled for terrorism... and this is a young American Colonel serving on an International Force."

I appreciated the President's sentiments and was sure that he was genuinely moved and concerned. But I wondered if he had any real idea of the depth of feelings shared by all the hostages' families.

Higgins' wife released what I thought was a particularly poignant statement. She had no idea what had happened to her husband. (I have always thought that it is better to know than not to know.) She said:

"I've seen reports and have not reached any conclusion myself. One thing I *have* learned over the past seventeen months is that the truth is hard to find and it remains so. But I am determined to know the truth."

She was a slim and attractive young woman, in the U.S. military herself. How her strong feelings echoed my own.

Of course, I listened attentively to the statements of all the international policy makers. In a television interview, Ehud Olmert, the Israeli cabinet minister, was asked to respond to a comment he had made earlier. "You had said something to the effect that American leaders tend to condemn publicly things like the kidnappings of that Shia group, but privately they are pleased with the result," he was told.

Olmert's reply, I thought, was evasive and purely, plainly, self-serving:

"...allow me to say first of all to express my condolences to the assault to the American colonel. We feel very sorry about these tragic events. And I also wish condolences to the American people and to [his] other family members.

"Even now we do not know if he [Higgins] was executed yesterday. But this is a very tragic event. However, one must understand, for Israel this is not a war that started yesterday. And, unfortunately, it may last for many years to come... this is a continuous battle that we have to face every day... and we are the main targets for these terrorists. Israelis are still hostage in Lebanon and they are trying to catch more."

I watched this program with dismay. To me it was just more diplomatic double-talk. It seemed to me that there were many more Lebanese held by the Israelis than the other way around. And what did his statement have to do with the American, British, and German hostages still being held? Israel had turned its back on them before. I prayed that they would now face them and hold out a hand that might bring them back to freedom.

Naturally, I was in regular contact with Joseph's family in America. It is probably a terrible thing to say, but they were keeping a death watch, as I was. After all, the terrorists had carried out their threat to execute Colonel Higgins and had announced that Joseph would be next. But we tried, as bravely as we could, to reassure one another. We promised to pray, to keep our faith in God, never to doubt that Joseph would be spared and that someday we would see him walking as a free man again. He would find himself in the bosom of a family that loved him.

I had not slept for days during the crisis and had eaten very little. I was exhausted with what seemed to be a fruitless effort to reach the people who were holding my husband. I was prepared to make any sacrifice in order for them to lift the death sentence they had imposed on him.

I called and asked the Lebanese television station if I could make a direct appeal to Joseph's captors. I was hoping that it would be broadcast world-wide, and might even reach some high officials in a remote corner of the Middle East who might be able to help us.

I can hardly remember being led into the building where the broadcast was to take place. I kept trying to think of what I would say, of how I could reach the hearts of the people who had condemned my husband.

There were some questions at first. The usual ones, such as, "How are you holding up, Mrs. Cicippio?" Then I faced the camera and spoke directly to the kidnappers. As I watched a rebroadcast later, I hoped and prayed that someone was watching who would show us some mercy.

"Please," I said, "Don't execute him. Please. That's all I want to tell them. That's all." Watching it later I thought how inadequate I had been. But what more could I possibly have said?

Then I was allowed a moment to speak directly to my husband. "Joe, my dearest," I said, "I know the situation in which we are. But all I ask you is to keep your hopes high. And don't ever lose faith in God. I'm sure that He won't leave us." It was a prepared statement, of course, but it was from my heart. I had no strong feeling that it would have any effect on the hostage-takers, but I hoped that someone—anyone in a position to help—might be able to take down the sword that was hanging over my husband's head.

Later there was a televised press conference with reporters from all over the world. I tried to explain that I wasn't there to attract attention to myself. I was only there to seek help from anyone, anywhere, who could help us. One reporter said there must be a way through diplomatic channels to save Joseph's life—as if we hadn't tried everything!

I told him, "If you can help me, please, go ahead. I'm asking the whole world, if there is anyone of you that still can help, please do it." Then I made an appeal to Mrs. Obeid, who was suffering through this ordeal as painfully as I was.

I felt so powerless. I never imagined that my television appeal would reach the heart of anyone, although one friend told me later that it had reduced him to tears. I was moved by his sentiment, but I didn't need tears. I needed help.

I was staying at the American Embassy then, in a small apartment they had provided to all the embassy personnel who were living on the West side of Beirut. But I was in my office when an international television station called and told me they had a videotape of Joseph making a statement. If I would go down to the station and consent to an interview, they would allow me to see it. They told me that I couldn't have the tape unless I agreed to personally pick it up and appear for their cameras.

I refused to be used, and finally they relented. If someone would come to the station, they said, they would let them have a copy of the tape. I called the ambassador and asked him if he would consider getting the tapes, but his response was negative. Once again I felt on my own, but surrounded by many good friends. Some friends, colleagues of mine, volunteered to go to the station and collect the videotape. The trip was always somewhat perilous because it meant you had to cross the Green Line that divided East and West Beirut, and there were still warring factions everywhere. I went with them and waited in the car. I was deeply grateful to them.

Finally, we returned with the tape and watched it in the apartment of one of my friends. The terrifying moment came when Joseph's poor, tired face, so drawn and haggard, appeared on the television screen. I was so happy to see him alive, even in that condition, that I almost leaped out of my chair. I cried with deep sorrow and wondered what tomorrow would hold for us and which miracle would happen to bring Joseph back to freedom and put an end to our sufferings.

I listened over and over to the statement they had prepared for him, every moment just wanting to reach out and touch him, to ease the sadness I saw in his expression. He said:

"I appeal to each person having honor, who can release Sheikh Abdul Karim Obeid, don't be late... because they are very serious to hang us and the period becomes very soon and the hour very little. My dear, and people, and all the American society and especially the Red Cross, don't leave me. And demand from the American people to oblige Israel to release Sheikh Karim Obeid immediately, because this is not human. We, the American people, are always the victim of Israel's politics. And President Bush has not helped to free us."

I knew it wasn't really Joe speaking. The language and many of the sentiments he uttered were totally unlike him. But then he added something that I knew was spoken from his heart, whether they had written the words for him or not. He seemed to look directly into my heart, to be reaching out to me with a gentle, consoling hand as he spoke:

"My dear wife. If you don't hear my voice and see my face again, I want you to look after yourself. And don't be sad. And always remember me."

This time I really broke down. The gentle hands of my friends patted my back, their soft murmuring voices offering me sympathy and encouragement.

That night I talked to Joseph's family in America. We tried to console each other and agreed to continue our prayers and not to let our hopes down. They had seen the broadcast, huddled around the television set in Thomas Cicippio's living room, and were as distressed as I was. But Thomas, Joseph's brother, was the strong one. He said that Joseph was strong, he would survive. Something would happen to make the terrorists change their position. Later, he confessed to me that he was so upset by the broadcast, seeing how emaciated Joseph looked, that he wasn't even sure it was his brother making the statement. It was not until he watched it many times that he became convinced that it was, indeed, the younger brother for whom he had such love and affection.

The first promising moment arrived when the kidnappers issued a statement that said they would extend the deadline for execution by another forty-eight hours. It wasn't deliverance, but it gave us another breath of hope.

Chapter 7

Joseph: I had no idea of what was happening. I didn't know that Sheikh Obeid had been abducted by the Israelis, that Colonel Higgins had been executed. I was never given the smallest sign, not the slightest suggestion, that I was a condemned hostage. For almost three years I had been completely shut off from the outside world.

Intuitively, I was able to guess that some events were going on that greatly displeased my captors. Once a guard came into our room and started slapping me around. It was completely unprovoked and I was astonished, totally taken by surprise. No words were spoken, just slap after slap to my face and the top of my head.

I wondered what I had done to enrage him so. I had made every effort to get along with the guards, to respond promptly to their orders, and to keep my distance to the extent I could do so whenever they seemed to be particularly agitated. So why this sudden and unprovoked assault?

Later I was to realize that it had occurred around the time of the Obeid incident. In the days that followed, the guard seemed almost chastened by what he had done. I remained silent and unprotesting, always careful to avoid his eyes.

Then they came for me. It was around four o'clock in the morning. Their flashlights scanned the walls of our room and then one shone directly into my eyes.

"Get up, Cicippio," one of them said. "We need you."

I sat up dazed and completely bewildered. What was happening now?

Another guard prodded me with a pistol. "Quickly," he said, "prepare yourself. Wash your face. We have a statement we want you to read."

I stood at the small basin in a corner of the room splashing water on my face, confused. A statement, he had said. But to whom? And what would I have to say? Certainly I wouldn't be allowed to express any of my own feelings, my own sentiments. I hoped it wouldn't be a vicious diatribe that excoriated the West, that maligned my own country. I hoped, too, that I might be able to say a few encouraging words to my wife, to my family. In a sense, the statement I was about to make contained both. But in any case I was obliged to say what they wanted me to say. I couldn't protest without inviting a severe beating or worse.

After I finished washing up, I was unchained, a towel was thrown over my head, and I was led from the room. When the towel was removed I found myself in an almost blindingly bright light. I noticed a TV camera mounted on a tall tripod and a technician standing behind it, feigning indifference. He acted as though it was just another job for him, just another night's work.

The camera light was killed and I was handed a script. "Read it exactly as it is written," one of them said, "nothing else."

I read the somewhat awkward statement and hoped that no one would actually believe I had authored it or that it expressed my true feelings or opinions, except where it spoke of my devotion to Elham. I wished they would allow me to add a few remarks to my family in America, my sons, my sisters and brothers, all the people for whom I felt such deep and abiding love.

During my first reading of the statement, I became quickly aware that I might be about to recite my own obituary. I had no idea who Sheikh Obeid was, no knowledge of the events that had brought me to that moment. But I had no doubt that my life was on the bargaining table, and that if something wasn't done I might be hanged later that morning.

When I spoke to my wife and urged her to get on with her life, I meant it sincerely. The words were theirs but the feelings were mine. Of course they had been written in an attempt to appeal to the emotions of everyone in the Western world. To suggest to the people, in America particularly, that here was a man their government had abandoned and whom they were perfectly willing to sacrifice. A man with a loving wife and family, whose only crime was to remain in Beirut. It was only the perfidy of the Israelis and their Western supporters that caused this man to come to such a tragic end.

In reading the statement, I sometimes found it difficult to disagree with parts of it, but of course it was nothing more than a carefully prepared propaganda piece.

They made me read it aloud three or four times before they were satisfied and placed me in front of the camera. One of them was kneeling just in front of me, holding cards with the words printed boldly on them. When I spoke the words "because they are very serious to hang us..." it came to me with a rush of feeling. I realized it was precisely what they intended to do. If some of their demands weren't met, especially the release of Sheikh Obeid, I was a dead man.

After the taping was over, the towel was placed over my head once again and I was taken back to my room. I did not sleep the rest of that morning, expecting that at any moment those dark, hooded men would burst into the room and sweep me away to my execution site. I thought of Elham and my family, praying that they would remember me. I asked forgiveness for my sins, for any wrongs I might have done to anyone in my life. Once more, I reached into the depths of my soul for the strength and courage I would need to face my death. The Twenty-third Psalm ran through my mind, "Yea, though I walk through the valley of the shadow of death I will fear no evil..."

Finally, I knew when it was morning and that dark night had passed. I would learn later that my captors had delayed my execution by forty-eight hours. Still, I lived in a constant state of anxiety. What had happened? What was the world up to?

Two days later, one of the guards handed me a picture and article cut from a local newspaper. The photo was of Elham! Anxiously, I asked what the article said. The guard smiled and said, "Your wife is a very courageous woman. She wants to say how much she loves you." I treasured that photograph and tried to handle it as delicately as possible. To me it was like a rare and beautiful bird. There were times when I held it to my breast before opening my hands to look down into her sad and lovely face.

I now believe that my wife's impassioned plea to my captors had everything to do with my deliverance. I think that her appearance on television to plead for my life and the words that she spoke reached their hearts and gave us the precious hours they needed to continue negotiating.

Chapter 8

Elham: First, we had to sit wringing our hands for forty-eight hours. The time seemed to pass so, so swiftly. I could think of nothing but poor Joseph. After his video statement, I knew he was aware of the desperate situation he was in, but I knew, also, how strong he was and that he would bravely accept whatever God had decided for him. My heart told me that he would face whatever happened with great courage, much more than I could summon if the terrorists were to carry out their threats. I thought that would be the end of me as well.

The hours ticked down to minutes and then the revolutionary group announced that they had extended the deadline for another forty-five minutes. Less than an hour! And yet it gave me the hope that something was going on behind the scenes that I could know nothing of.

It was the intervention of Rafsanjani that ended the crisis. He had been elected president of Iran that month, just two months after the death of Ayatollah Khomeini. Rafsanjani deplored the death of Colonel Higgins and in a prayer meeting in Teheran he said:

"I address the White House. There is a solution for Lebanon, a solution for freeing the hostages. Take a sensible attitude and we will help to solve the problems there so the people of the region may live in peace and friendship."

This was said only the day after Rafsanjani took office and to me it seemed like a divine intervention. Right after this address, Sheikh Mohammed Hussein Fadlallah urged his followers to be "more loftier," more humanitarian. Fadlallah was the head of the Hezbollah, the "Party of God," and a very powerful influence in the underground groups that were still active in Lebanon.

At last, the Revolutionary Justice Organization sent a note

to a news agency in Beirut stating that the execution had been frozen indefinitely.

I was filled with sudden, exhilarating joy. When we received the news, my friends, my colleagues at the embassy embraced each other, weeping with happiness. And now I remembered my confidence in God and deep belief in Joseph's kindness. It had helped me to endure all those terrible hours and days. I felt, more strongly than ever, that one day Joseph would be free. As I had felt the urge to call for a press conference when Joseph's life was in danger, I then felt an obligation to appear again and thank all those who had helped to spare Joseph's life.

I had excited, joyous talks with Joseph's family in America. They had suffered, of course, as painfully as I had. We all felt as though a great, dark cloud had been lifted from above us.

Chapter 9

Joseph: For some days after I had been forced to make the video statement, there was an electric tension in the air. I noticed that the guards kept averting their eyes, not really wanting to look at me as they went about their daily routine. I imagine it's the same in the death ward of a prison; nobody really wants to look at a man who is condemned and about to die.

Once I had survived that terrible first night, I tried to resume my daily regimen. I was able to exercise, though without my usual enthusiasm. I would try to lose myself in the words of Emily Brontë, or in the heady, adventurous world of Robin Hood. I searched for some encouragement in the beautiful and inspiring words of the Koran. The words often became a blur. The idea that I was destined for the gallows kept intruding into my mind.

I remember seeing a French film that depicted condemned prisoners in the Bastille. After a prisoner's appeal had been denied, the guards would rush into a cell that held eight or ten men and, without warning, grab the lost man and take him out to be executed. The other convicts would sigh with relief. It wasn't their turn this time. But if the guards were to suddenly burst into my room, I would know instantly who they were coming for. I prepared myself to make one last statement, although I had no real conviction that they would allow it. The last address I would make had already been spoken and the words had come from the mouths of my captors. And then, I wondered, what would they do with Edward Tracy? Would they hang him as well, a poor soul who, I believe, had never done harm to anyone? Whenever I tried to reach out to God, Edward was always in my prayers.

Exactly when it happened I can't say, but a few days after I made the videotape, the mood seemed to shift almost imperceptibly. The guards seemed to look at me more directly, and behind their hooded masks I could almost sense a small smile. I began to breathe more evenly and resumed my self-imposed regimen with renewed hope and energy. Outside of knowing that a sheikh named Obeid was a central figure in what I thought must be an international crisis, I was unaware of anything that was going on in the world around me. For whatever reasons they had, my captors told me nothing. I think it was their way of trying to keep my mind an empty vessel, and me obedient, submissive, and always responsive to whatever demands they made of me, like a trained dog. I would sit up and bark if they demanded it. I would extend my paw in friendliness, if they might accept it. I would try to satisfy my hunger with whatever meager dishes they put in front of me. I would even, silently, endure the switch. But I was a man, not a dog. And I don't think they could comprehend the strength that I had kept hidden inside me and that was growing day by day.

I had learned, for example, that silence can be a very effective way of communicating with another human being. When a guard came into the room to offer me a small supper, I would accept it gratefully, without words. If they took me to the bathroom, I followed without complaint and only spoke if I was asked a direct question, which was not often.

This, of course, was a particular indignity, since I had to perform whatever bodily functions were necessary in the presence of a guard. But I learned to become almost indifferent to it. The guards, I suspect, might almost have been as embarrassed as I was. In time, it became just another routine. The guard would stand with his back to me, and I would respond as quickly as I could. I was never punished for staying in the "loo," as the British call it, too long.

For a while there were four other hostages with us, whose faces I never saw, but I believe them to be Professors Polhill, Steen, Turner, and Singh. One of them was severely ill with dysentery, and it seemed that I was always to follow him into the bathroom.

It is not the most polite subject to talk about, but I think it's important in order to describe the conditions in which we were being held.

The Arabic toilet is infinitely more practical than the Western versions. It is simply a kind of decorative, accommodating hole in the floor, surrounded by tile. A water tap is within hands' reach, an aspect of the Arab insistence on cleanliness.

One morning, I was led into the bathroom just after the sick man had left. I was dismayed. I pleaded with the guard to let me have some cleansers, paper towels, anything he could provide. He returned, smiling, I suspected, behind his hooded mask, and offered me a package of brushes, cleansers, and whatever was necessary.

I devoted myself to the daily chore of keeping the bathroom clean and sanitary. I suppose I became what the army would call a latrine orderly, although performing the task didn't make me feel any less about myself. In fact, it gave me the encouragement to further convince myself that I was a useful human being. However insignificant or ignominious this daily task might seem to some people, it at least gave me the feeling that, by this small gesture, I was doing something for my fellow man.

Humility doesn't mean abject surrender. It means simply confronting the fact that we are all a part of this world, this universe, and that often the greatest gift we can give to the world is the kindest and most generous part of ourselves. We will always be the benefactors of whatever small help and encouragement we can offer to another. Humility isn't a weakness, it is a true expression of strength.

Cleaning the bathroom was a blessing, in a way. I came to understand the biblical story of Christ kneeling to wash the feet of the apostles, and while in no way did I feel Christ-like, I felt that I had come to understand the story's deepest meaning.

Students changing classes at noontime on the campus of the American University of Beirut, October 1984. *Credit: Cicippio Collection*

American University of Beirut campus. *Credit: Cicippio Collection*

Elham and I are engaged! March 1985. *Credit: Cicippio Collection*

Joe Cicippio in Beirut on the American University campus, 1986. *Credit: Cicippio Collection*

Elham with Edward and Mary Brown, Joseph's best and oldest friends.
Credit: Cicippio Collection

Elham with Frances and Thomas Cicippio, meeting Joseph's family in 1987.
Credit: Cicippio Collection

American University of Beirut before the explosion of 1991.
Credit: Cicippio Collection

Clock from the top of College Hall after an explosion on the American
University of Beirut campus in November 1991. *Credit: Cicippio Collection*

The City of Philadelphia's lights welcomed me home as I drove from the airport to my home outside the city. *Credit: Cicippio Collection*

Emotional meeting with sister Helen Fazio on return home.
Credit: Cicippio Collection

Joseph with brother Tom and his famous signs. *Credit: Cicippio Collection*

A visit to Valley Forge Park with Elham shortly after my return home. *Credit: Cicippio Collection*

Ceremony of Arlington Cemetery for hostages who were killed, sponsored by Carmella LaSpoda of "No Greater Love" at left with Terry Anderson. *Credit: Cicippio Collection*

A meeting of former hostages in Washington. First row left to right: Father Lawrence Martin Jenco, Rev. Benjamin Weir, Terry Anderson, Thomas Sutherland, Joseph Cicippio. Back row left to right: Alann Steen, Mithileshwor Singh, Frank Regier, David Jacobsen, David Dodge, Robert Polhill. *Credit: Cicippio Collection*

Commencement speaker at Seton Hall University School of Law, where I was awarded an Honorary Degree in Law. *Credit: Cicippio Collection*

On the occasion of my receiving an honorary degree, Seton Hall University School of Law, New Jersey, June 1992. On my right is the Very Reverend Thomas Peterson, Chancellor, and on my left, the Most Reverend Theodore E. McCarrick, Ph.D., D.D., Archbishop of Newark. *Credit: Cicippio Collection*

Al and Betty Cicippio at their 50th wedding anniversary in June 1988. Al is Joseph's oldest brother and role model since childhood.
Credit: Cicippio Collection

Joseph and Elham with Helen Fazio, his sister, who willed herself to live until his release.
Credit: Cicippio Collection

Governor of New Jersey, Jim Florio, and wife greeting the Cicippios at their home at Eastertime, where Elham witnessed her first Easter egg hunt on the Florio's front lawn.
Credit: Cicippio Collection

A meeting with Col. Oliver North.
Credit: Cicippio Collection

National Committee on American Foreign Policy luncheon in New York to honor H.E. Javier Perez de Cuellar (center), Sec. Gen., United Nations; with Giandomenico Picco, Assistant Secretary, U.N.; Nobel Laureate Elie Wiesel; and the Cicippios. *Credit: Cicippio Collection*

Donald Trump with Marla Maples and the Cicippios at Trump Castle in Atlantic City, New Jersey. Donald Trump was one of the first to welcome me on my return to America. *Credit: Cicippio Collection*

Lebanese orphans at our home in Princeton, December 1986.
Credit: Cicippio Collection

Elham and Joseph with Nicholas Issa, a Lebanese orphan who was fitted with prosthetic arm while visiting America. *Credit: Cicippio Collection*

Nicholas Issa with Frank Malone, being fitted with prosthetic arm. *Credit: Cicippio Collection*

William Flynn, Rose Bowl Assistant Executive Director (center), with Joseph and Skip Oliver, lawyer, (left) and Bob Johnson, Joseph's Rose Bowl escort for a week (right). *Credit: Cicippio Collection*

Grand Marshall U.S. Senator Ben "Knighthorse" Campbell; Robert L. Cheney, President, Pasadena Tournament of Roses; Co-Grand Marshall Christo Columbus, direct descendent of the famous explorer; and Joseph. *Credit: Cicippio Collection*

Joseph on a Pasadena
Tournament of Roses float.
Credit: Cicippio Collection

Elham helping to
decorate float.
Credit: Cicippio Collection

Elham and I taking a walk in Florida as guests of the American Trial Lawyer's Association. *Credit: Cicippio Collection*

Chapter 10

Elham: The hostage crisis was a terrible strain on everyone in the Cicippio family. And during the time that Joseph was held captive, they had to endure other tragedies as well.

Joseph's oldest son, Joseph, Jr., who had worked so tirelessly for his father's freedom, died suddenly of a massive heart attack.

Both of Joseph's sisters, Rose and Helen, were diagnosed with terminal cancer. Despite her brave effort to survive, Rose died before she could ever see her brother again. Helen, who often said that good news about her brother was far better for her health than all of the many chemotherapy treatments she had had to undergo, was determined to live until Joseph was free. Joseph's son David said that Helen was full of energy and refused to give up until her brother was safely home again.

Thomas was a tower of strength, which inspired everyone in the family. Each evening, winter and summer, he would go out on the lawn of his house and change the sign that numbered the days all the hostages had been kept in captivity. His spirit never wavered. He never stopped believing that one day his brother would be released.

And there had come to be more than just a flickering light at the end of a long, dark tunnel. Rafsanjani publicly declared that the hostage problem would be solved and, as we knew, he had the power to do it.

The financial support for the Hezbollah had come almost entirely from Iran, and without it, they would be almost powerless. Rafsanjani had quickly solved the in-fighting that had divided so many factional groups in Iran. He also had direct contact with Imad Mugniyeh, a Shia Muslim who was in a strong position of leadership among the Lebanese hostage-takers.

I followed the news constantly, always hoping that I would hear some encouraging words about Joseph. The situation had been a constant nightmare for so many years, and now it seemed that things were changing. I prayed that they would be for the better.

The *Teheran Times*, which was totally controlled by the Iranian government, published an article saying that Iran would work to free the hostages if the United States would release billions of dollars in Iranian assets that had been frozen in American banks at the time of the Iranian Revolution. Of course, this was Rafsanjani talking, and he spoke again in another editorial published in the *Teheran Times* in February of 1990. The article called for the release of all hostages without any conditions. Shortly after, Rafsanjani made a public statement that 1990 might be the year that all the hostages would be freed. He said, "My feeling is that the issue of the hostages is moving toward a solution." Naturally, he was trying to fix the blame on American policy when he added, "...the U.S. and others are exploiting the matter as a means of branding the Lebanese as terrorists."

They were not the most generous words he might have uttered. He expressed no sympathy for the innocent hostages and the terrible conditions in which they were being held. But at least a dialogue had begun. I prayed that it would continue. I did not want to face further endless months and years without knowing anything about Joseph's fate. That was the torment the Hezbollah had imposed on me.

If my husband had been a criminal, sentenced and put away for a certain period of time, I would at least have known where he was and when he might be released. But Joseph was an innocent man, generous and kind to everyone, who had been cruelly taken from me. I will always remember the long days and nights I spent alone without his reassuring presence, wondering what his thoughts were and wishing I could be wherever he was being held, to console and comfort him. Just a brief note—a simple message to tell me he was all right—from Joseph would have given me great joy. The Hezbollah might easily have done this, a simple, kind act that would have done so much to restore my spirit. But I never received a word, and was often left to stare at dark, empty walls in rooms that seemed so lifeless without him.

It wasn't always easy to keep my faith alive. There were times when I almost resigned myself to the thought that I would never see him again. But then I would suddenly find myself believing, more strongly than ever, that I would see him safe with his family and loved ones. I experienced powerful feelings—almost like messages from God—that my devotion and the constant prayers of Joseph's family in America would someday be answered.

Without faith, I don't think any of us could have survived those critical times. We had met with what seemed like indifference whenever we tried to approach an official we thought might be able to help us. Such people would express great sympathy, tell us how saddened they were, and that everything was being done that could be done. We must simply be patient and wait. Then we would receive a small encouraging pat on the shoulder and be sent on our way if, indeed, we were able to see the person in the first place. (There were many closed doors.)

And so I returned to my empty apartment and tried to live with my grief and sorrow through another dark night. The only hope I had was to reach into the heavens and beg the Almighty for deliverance.

My heart quickened with hope in April 1990, when Robert Polhill, who had been a teacher at the Beirut University College, was released. He was one of four academics held by the Islamic Jihad for the Liberation of Palestine. Mr. Polhill made few comments after his release, which was very frustrating for me, since I had hoped he might have some news about Joseph. Later, I would learn that he had a painfully sore throat condition that turned out to be cancerous. I could only feel sorrow for the man.

A week later, another ray of hope: Frank Reed, who directed the Lebanese International School and had been taken by the Organization of Islamic Dawn, was to be released in twenty-four hours. He was driven, as promised, to the American Embassy in Damascus and was described as being in good health, despite his ordeal. Nothing had been heard from Reed since September 1986, the same month that Joseph had been kidnapped.

Such fantastic news! I couldn't help feeling that Joseph would be the next to be released, and I spent long hours near the telephone hoping to hear his voice, telling me that we would meet again soon, that he was free and well. It was all I could think about. Once again I would undergo a crushing disappointment.

The months dragged on with no news of Joseph.

In August of 1990, Iraqi President Saddam Hussein drove his army into Kuwait. His aim was to take control over Middle East oil, which would give him total control of the area.

The attack allowed the seventeen Dawa prisoners held in Kuwait to escape. The Dawas were Shia Muslims who had staged a series of attacks against the American and French Embassies in Kuwait. First, a truck carrying 45 cylinders of gas, attached to plastic explosives, had rammed into the administrative annex, reducing it to rubble. If the driver had not missed the main chancellery, there would have been a devastating loss of life.

An hour later a car bomb exploded outside the French Embassy, almost killing the ambassador when the explosion sent a large crystal chandelier crashing down on his desk.

The greatest devastation would have happened if the terrorists had succeeded in blowing up Kuwait's desalination plant, which would have left the desert area without water. The fire would have burned for years. But the suicide driver, for some unknown reason, blew up his explosives and himself 150 yards short of the target.

But since they had escaped, the seventeen Dawa prisoners were no longer an issue in the hostage negotiations. The Shia Muslims had demanded their release before they would consider setting any of the hostages free.

Also, the U.S. air attack had given Iran more reason then ever to meet with the West at the bargaining tables. Their eight-year war with Iraq was still going on, and now Iran and the Western nations had a common enemy. They made strange bedfellows.

That same month, the Northern Irish hostage, Brian Keenan, was released after more than four years as a hostage. I felt a strong, new resurgence of hope.

Chapter 11

Joseph: I had no idea that the Desert Storm operation was going on, although I thought I detected some excited exchanges among the guards. I was very curious, of course. But it was only after my release that I learned that I was being held by an Iranian-based terrorist group. There is no question what my fate would have been had I been held by Iraqis.

So much was happening in the outside world that I would have given anything to know about. Almost every event in the Middle East had some powerful effect on my situation. Learning about the events filled days and weeks of my time after I was released, and the more I learned the more I wondered why my country couldn't have done more to gain the freedom of the American hostages, or of all the hostages. While captive, however, I lived in a vacuum, with one day much like the other, never knowing anything outside my small room. There were times when I felt the world had totally abandoned me. Then I would remember the devotion of my wife, and the love and sharing that had always been such a strong part of my family in America. I knew I was not alone, and that conviction carried me through some of the darkest moments of my captivity.

I had come to realize, more clearly than ever, that there was a fire within me that needed only to be fueled by my own spirit. I had been threatened with imminent death many times as a hostage. But I recalled the lines written by the Welsh poet, Dylan Thomas:

> Do not go gently into that good night,
> Rage, rage against the dying of the light!

To me, that means that we should never meekly surrender God's greatest gift, which is life. I was resolved to survive, not by hating my captors, but by forgiving them. And to find the inner resolve to face, as calmly and as resolutely as

I could, whatever fate had prepared for me. I might be raging inside as they bound me and blindfolded me and placed the rough noose around my neck. But after my years of religious upbringing and my devoted reading of the Koran while a captive, I had developed a spiritual strength that no one could weaken. They might take my life, but they would not capture my soul.

The thought that some outside event might put me close to the gallows again never completely left my mind. I would watch the guards carefully when they entered our room to bring us food, trying to see if there was any shift in their behavior. I almost began to think I could see their faces through the black, forbidding masks they wore, but of course I would never really be able to identify a single one. And, except for a few, their voices were very much the same, usually gruff and commanding. I got the impression, at times, that they might be trying to disguise the way they spoke, as if fearing some future retribution. We gave some of them names, but only because of some peculiarity of manner or conduct. Sometimes they would order us to stand up and face the wall before they entered, and at such times I knew they were unmasked. Once or twice I was tempted to peek around, if for no other reason than to see another human face, but I knew what the consequence would be. A severe beating, or worse. I always kept my eyes fixed on the gray, cracked walls until I was sure the guards had left.

Remarkably, Edward Tracy did the same, as compliantly as I did, although he would mumble and mutter at the wall as though he were engaging in conversation with what was to me an unseen face, an unheard voice.

Edward's condition had worsened, month by month, year by year. There were times when he would be lucid for a few moments and then, without warning, he would retreat into his disordered mind and talk gibberish again. I so wished that he could be in a hospital where he could be treated for his unfortunate illness. But his only "doctors" were Shia guards, who had no sympathy for Tracy or his condition, and who had often beaten him for his uncontrollable behavior.

I confess there was a time when I wished Tracy were

freed to a world where he might be treated with kindness and understanding, where he might be cured of his illness. But then I would think of us as brothers, thrown together by circumstances that neither of us could have imagined a few years before.

Chapter 12

Elham: The end of the Lebanese Civil War came about when Gen. Michel Aoun stepped down in 1990. He had been a kind of self-imposed president of the country, and his promises had been unfulfilled. Now the Syrian army brought it's forces in and disarmed the local militias.

It was the end of the war and I rejoiced, hoping that this would be the end of the terrible pain that my people had endured for fifteen years. I wished that, finally, there would be a true healing process that would bring peace to that turbulent part of the world and freedom for Joseph.

I was encouraged when the British restored diplomatic relations with Iran in November of that year and Prime Minister Margaret Thatcher resigned. She had seemed so inflexible when it came to any dealings with the hostage-takers. Shortly after she stepped down, Douglass Hogg, the British foreign minister, flew to Beirut to meet Lebanese officials, who gave him assurances that all the British hostages would be freed. Roger Cooper, a British journalist who had spent five years in an Iranian prison on charges of espionage, had already been released a month earlier. And then in August of 1991, the doors were opened to another British news writer, John McCarthy. He had been kidnapped on his way to the Beirut airport in 1986, supposedly sold out to the Hezbollah by one of his own men for $100,000.

Whatever reason they had to abduct McCarthy was never made clear, except that at the time, any Englishman was fair game for the hostage-takers. It was after the American bombing of Libya, and Quadaffi was supposed to have offered the Islamic Jihad $30 million for the American hostages. They had refused, wanting to keep their captives for what they thought was a higher political purpose.

My heart goes out to McCarthy, who had been treated so brutally while a captive and whose mother had died before she could see her son again or even be told he was alive. Many terrible wounds were inflicted on the hostages' families by the Hezbollah.

Now at last I heard that Joseph was to be released! It was so exciting for me. Such wonderful news! The newspaper statement said that Joseph would be dropped at the Beaurivage Hotel in West Beirut. I packed a suitcase, thinking I would be going on to Wiesbaden in Germany with Joseph, and after a few days we would be flying to the United States.

My hands were trembling as I opened the lid of my suitcase and began to fill it with my clothes. I thought such foolish things: Would Joseph like the way I was dressed, the way I was made up, would he even remember what I looked like? I was like a bride about to go on her honeymoon. I felt such great relief, such great joy that the nightmare was over at last and that I would be with my husband again after so many lost years.

I sat in the car that would take me to the hotel, pressing my hands together in prayerful thanks to God for allowing me this wonderful moment.

When my brother and I reached the hotel, the lobby was filled with media people, local and international. We were all waiting as the promised time passed. We were wondering, when one of the reporters said, "I'm sorry, Mrs. Cicippio. The man they released was Edward Tracy. He was being held with your husband."

My heart stopped for a moment. I felt faint before my brother took my arm and led me to a chair.

"I'm sorry," I said. "But my hope was too high."

After recovering myself, I realized that, although I had to deal with another disappointment, at least we were going in the right direction—another hostage out. I went home totally shattered. My father, with his weak, sick voice, tried to cheer me up. The telephone rang from the embassy and a kind man spoke to me gently. It was Ambassador Ryan Crocker, the sweetest person I have ever met. We talked for a while. The second morning I went to the embassy as usual and tried to regain my strength once more. I met with the ambassador and he updated me with Tracy's condition and promised to report every news item related to Joseph.

"May I speak to Mr. Tracy?" I asked. I was desperate for any news of my husband. "I'm afraid not, Mrs. Cicippio," he said. Tracy is in a very bad mental state, not really aware of what has happened to him, although he did say that Joseph is in a good physical condition." When he saw that I looked down at my hands, clenched together, he added, "Please don't despair. I'm sure your husband will be with you soon."

The ambassador was a kind man, but after so many false promises, so many dashed hopes, whom could I believe anymore? In the car ride back to the apartment, I felt, for the first time, a deep bitterness. It was not because Edward Tracy had been released instead of Joseph. I had only sympathy for Tracy. But I confess that I felt some concern that Joseph and he had been held together for so long. I had heard from friends and acquaintances in Beirut, who had known Tracy before he was kidnapped, that he had been mentally ill before the terrorists took him from the sidewalk cafe in West Beirut. "He was around the bend," as one confidant put it. It made me fear for Joseph, until I realized that my good and kind husband would find a way to deal with it.

When I got back to the empty apartment, I put my bag in a corner of the room, wondering how many times I would have to pack and unpack my suitcase before Joseph would be really released. I wouldn't open it until days later. That night I watched Tracy's press conference on television. He spoke of how well he had been treated, and of how they had even been served luxurious food, even chateaubriand. I was very happy to hear that, but it was hard to believe.

Chapter 13

Joseph: When Edward was finally released in August of 1991, I was, quite honestly, relieved. I have nothing but the greatest affection for the man and was sorrowful that he was in such a sad condition.

There were times when he would talk lucidly to me for a few moments, and then lapse into a totally incomprehensible monologue, the meaning of which was known only to himself. I would try to cajole him, to bring him back to reality. "Come on, Edward," I would say, "get out of Disneyland."

His expression would contort into some kind of half-smile, he would mutter something unintelligible, crawl back into his pallet, and pull the thin blanket over his head, still moaning and mumbling.

If I ever felt pity for myself, I had only to look at Tracy to realize what true misery is really like. I think that a severe mental illness is one of the saddest tragedies inflicted on mankind.

At least I had some rational idea of why I was a hostage, who my captors were, and where I was being held. Edward had only the vaguest idea. If you had told him that he was being held on an alien planet by the Mormon Tabernacle Choir, he might have believed it. Then he would have simply retreated into the world that he or someone or something had created for him. Oh, how often I mourned for him.

But now I had cause to celebrate for my poor friend. Late in the evening, several guards came into our room. They told me to lie flat on my pallet and face the wall. They covered me with a blanket. I could hear the sounds of movement, of bodies stirring, but no words were spoken.

After about ten minutes, a guard came in and removed the blanket. I waited for the familiar click of the door being locked, and then looked around. Edward was gone. His mat and blankets had been folded against the wall. I was alone.

I was happy for him. And not just because I would no longer have to endure his irrational behavior. After more than four years I had become almost accustomed to it. Looking after Edward as well as I could, and to the extent that he would allow it, had become an occupation for me. If there is such a thing as a paramedic in a psychiatric ward, I was one.

But I was also happy for myself. Tracy's release encouraged me to believe that my own freedom was not too distant. It began to take on an almost palpable shape, and images of Elham danced in my mind. I imagined seeing a clear, blue sky again, a bright, sunlit day, nights when the heavens were filled with tiny, glittering stars. I thought of sitting down with my family and sharing a delightfully cooked meal with them. Of embracing my sisters, my brothers, my children, everyone whom I had known and loved. Of being able to simply take a stroll whenever I felt like it. Of seeing a movie or watching a television show. Of listening to music, or reading a book of my own choice. They weren't particularly romantic fantasies, only things that most of us take for granted. But I had been deprived of them for many long years. Now I felt that I wouldn't exchange those ordinary, day-to-day pleasures for all the wealth in the world. I had been a materialistic man, but through meditation and constant inward searching during my captivity, I had come to believe that the greatest rewards in life are the simplest: that freedom, not just of the body, but of the mind and soul and spirit, is everything. It was a lesson I had been compelled to learn through very bitter experience.

With Tracy gone, I was alone—but with a strength and hope that my captors could not diminish. My one fear was that the guards would lead him back into the room and announce that it was all a mistake, that he would not be released after all. After a few days, however, I began to believe that they had either shot him for some imagined crime or that he had truly been repatriated. I preferred to believe the latter, of course, but I still remembered Normandin's warning never to accept as truth anything the terrorists told us.

Three days after the release of Edward Tracy, the officer in charge of my guards came in with a local newspaper showing Edward in a picture speaking to reporters. I was informed that Edward was on his way home. I was asked what my feelings were now that Edward had been released before me. I answered that I was greatly relieved, and that my own captivity would be much easier to handle—any problems which then arose would be of my own making.

I was also informed that a deal had been struck with Israel. Edward Tracy would be released first in exchange for Sheikh Abdul Karim Obeid, who would then be released the following weekend. Following Sheikh Obeid's release, I would be released within the next few days. The following weekend came and went with no release of Sheikh Obeid. The guards said that perhaps there had been a mix-up, and the release of Sheikh Obeid would occur a week later. But even then, no Sheikh Obeid. Eventually the guards informed me that Israel had not kept its agreement and I was not going to be released.

My life continued in vermin-ridden confinement. It would take an entomologist to name the variety of insects that assailed me day and night. One species was the tarantula, a hairy, long-legged beast whose bite was extremely painful, but seldom fatal. I had to constantly brush them off my clothing, so aggressive were they. There were other bugs as well that were almost beyond description. Big ones, small ones, black, gray, multi-colored—they came arrogantly marching into my room whenever they felt like it, usually at night. I might be reading a book and discover one or two marching across the page before I was able to brush them away. My mind would instantly snap back from a beautiful imagined scene in England to the awful confines in which I was being held. The insects would crawl up the sleeves of my running suit or somehow find their way inside my pants' legs. It was a constant war, especially at night. And they didn't come singly or in pairs. They came in battalions.

Then there were the rats. I have a friend who was in Korea during the war, and he described the rats that invaded his bunker as being the size of beavers. The rats that came to my room were no less formidable. And when the rats were away, the mice came out to play. I don't know if there is a pecking order in the rodent family, but that is the way it appeared to me.

The guards were sympathetic. I suspect they were tortured by the animals and insects as much as I was. Yet everything they tried to do was unsuccessful. I sometimes thought that what we needed was a good American exterminator. But the house we were in had probably been unoccupied for such a long time before our arrival as captives that the vermin had simply taken over. Trying to maintain my positive attitude, I reasoned that bug-swatting and rat-catching were just other ways of filling the empty hours.

I sometimes felt like the biblical Job—that God had given me this painful trial to test my faith and spirit.

And now I was about to face one more painful ordeal.

Chapter 14

Elham: It isn't the kind of thing you can prepare yourself for: Joseph's abduction—the uncertainty of not knowing where he was, of how he was being treated, or even if he was alive—was a constantly painful experience. I lived with it day and night; it never left me.

I read every newspaper, watched every TV news report, tried to learn anything I could about my husband. Except for Normandin, all the released hostages knew nothing about Joseph, and Edward Tracy was completely out of touch with reality. I learned that three days after he had been flown to Wiesbaden for a medical checkup, he was sent to a psychiatric hospital in America. It was so sad for him. No one was there to meet him at the airport in Germany. He had led such a strange, wandering existence throughout Europe and the Middle East that he seemed never to have made any close relationships. I think Joseph may have been the closest friend he ever had.

It may seem strange that the best source of the little information that I could obtain about Joseph was the news media. The Hezbollah provided them with news about the hostages who were still being held, news I had been unable to get anywhere else.

I was searching through the paper hoping there might be some word of Joseph when I saw a small article that said he had been taken seriously ill and that he was in a hospital, being treated for a stomach ailment. My heart stopped. I knew he had suffered from some intestinal problems in the past, and I prayed that after all he had gone through, he would not meet the same fate as the CIA director, William Buckley. I know I use the word "prayer" quite often, but it was the only thing that sustained me, that kept my faith alive. When you are in such deep distress there is nothing stronger than your sincerity or more powerful than your belief.

I went as usual to Ambassador Crocker and asked him whether he had heard any news about Joseph being ill or if he could confirm or deny it. There was a long moment of silence, and then he said, "We really don't know." But I was able to look deep into his eyes, trying to avoid believing that Joseph was sick. I finally suggested that the kidnappers could have been trying to find an excuse to release Joseph by saying he was sick. There was nothing I could do but to put all my trust in what I believed, and continue to pray.

I don't believe that prayer is something you do exclusively for yourself alone, or for your family or loved ones. I think prayers must always include the suffering people in every part of the world. Without a sense of universal life, prayer becomes almost meaningless. And I suspect God doesn't answer selfish requests.

So I continued to pray for Joseph, and all the hostages.

Chapter 15

Joseph: I became ill in September of 1991, violently and painfully ill. I was stricken with terrible abdominal pain that left me weak and trembling. I couldn't stand or eat or sleep.

At first, the guards may have thought I was shamming, but then they saw how ill I was and summoned a doctor. Within a half-hour he was there beside my makeshift bed, probing and questioning.

It was odd to see a physician standing over me, his face concealed by a mask as he examined me. But I was so ill—my body shaking, the sweat pouring out of me—that I couldn't have recognized him in my delirium even if he were unmasked. When I asked him what was wrong with me, he shook his head, gravely I thought, and said nothing. It was not a very reassuring prognosis, nor did it give me any great confidence in the physician. Simply by his manner I could tell that he had some real concern about my condition. He was, after all, a doctor, and I think he took his calling seriously. He returned at times to see how I was, but I think he was unfamiliar with whatever had caused my illness or even what it was.

I lay that way, moving in and out of consciousness and in a delirium of pain, for four days. In a few clear moments I searched, once again within myself, to discover those resources of strength that would help me to survive. It was as though God had decided to test my faith and resolve one more time.

My captors finally brought in another physician who seemed to be more knowledgeable about my condition. I can never forget how gently his hands probed my body and how kind and concerned he seemed to be. I suspect that this doctor was a gastroenterologist and also a surgeon. He quickly ordered the guards to deliver me to a hospital. It was around 10 p.m. when they carried me out to a waiting automobile and carefully placed me in the trunk. Even in that cramped and painful position, I was grateful to be out of the steaming house where we had been kept for over two years. The ventilation there was almost nonexistent, and at times the heat was so overwhelming that I would find myself soaked through with perspiration and almost gasping for breath. How I had wished for a soft breeze and a few lungfuls of the cool air that blew in off the Mediterranean Sea. As they carried me to the waiting car, I tried to breathe in as much of it as I could. On every occasion that I was moved (except when I was stowed into a car trunk), I would inhale that wonderful elixir that we all take for granted. To me it was the fresh, clean air of freedom, and in the few, brief moments when I was moved from car to car or from a car to a new place of captivity, I wanted to absorb as much of it as I could.

Despite my physical condition, the Hezbollah used the same routine in taking me from the "Farm House" to the hospital as they had in moving me from one location to another, except that this time I think they were more concerned because of my illness. Try as I might, I wasn't always able to stifle a cry or smother a moan. I was in very deep pain, and they handled me as gently as they could. I was shifted four times that night before we arrived at the hospital. The trip had taken easily an hour.

I was blindfolded, of course, as I was placed on a gurney and wheeled into the operating room. Over and over I pleaded with them to let me know what was wrong with me, only to hear the small, echoing sounds of padded feet moving through the operating chamber, the clink of metal instruments, and the muted voices of doctors conferring together.

A doctor's voice said, "Sleep now, you will be all right." I

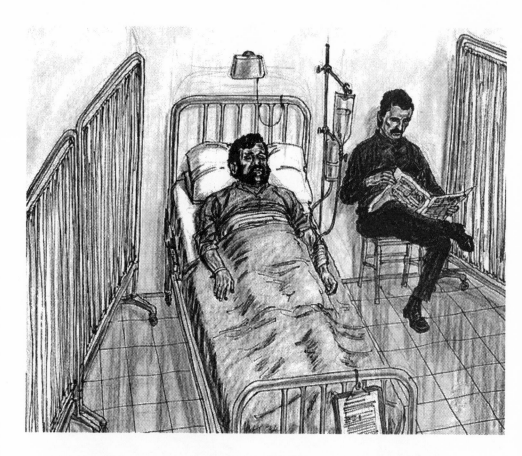

looked up at the bright overhead lights for a brief moment
before I sank into oblivion.

Through the days of my semidelirium, my mind had
been filled with thoughts of Elham. I remembered how
passionately she loved flowers, how every room in our
apartment was filled with the fragrance of freshly cut
blossoms, carefully and beautifully arranged by her. Visitors
often commented on how tastefully she had placed them,
how they filled the rooms with such elegance.

The flowers came to symbolize all the beauty I had lost,
and later I vowed to show Elham a nation that was exploding
with flowers instead of shells. I had half-forgotten visions of
the New Year's Day parade in Pasadena, the Parade of Roses,
but now I resolved to take her there if I survived—if I were
ever made a free man again.

After the operation I woke up in a strange room not really knowing where I was. My eyes were still covered and taped. I was able to make out images of IV stands, looming like silent sentinels on each side of my bed. The room appeared to be in semidarkness.

I was in a hospital room that was completely isolated from the other patients. And outside of a sense of weakness and a dull kind of post-operative ache in my abdomen, I felt very much better than the night they had transported me from the "Farm House" to the hospital.

Here I was treated with as much care and kindness as if I were a patient at Johns Hopkins or the Mayo Clinic, any fine American hospital, except that the people who looked after me were never able to reveal their identities. The surgeon who had performed the operation came in regularly to check on my condition. I wondered if he hadn't been an exchange student trained at some American medical facility, and if in these strange circumstances he were not expressing his gratitude. I will always remember his soft and gentle hands and the kindness with which he treated me.

My hospitalization also made me realize that the group that had taken me was no mere rogue organization. They were part of a vast, highly-skilled, government-supported network. They had to have been financially well supported, with excellent communications and access to anything they pleased.

After five days in the hospital, the guards came in one night and moved me to another location not far from there. I really believe that this move was at the insistence of the surgeon. I think he was a dedicated man who wanted only to look after the welfare of his patient. He was a doctor, after all.

The guards had to stand on either side of me and almost carry me to the automobile. I was still feeling some pain and discomfort, but was able to take a few halting steps.

Strangely, the guards were almost solicitous of me, as if they were taking home a close and loved relative who had just undergone a serious operation. "Careful," they would say. "Go slowly." Then I would recall the Koran and the Islamic devotion to the sick, the aged, and the infirm.

Considering the cruel butchery of the fifteen-year war, the horrifying deaths and disfigurements that had been visited on so many thousands of their people, this may seem an odd contradiction. But their faith is deep, their convictions profound. The Lebanese people and the Islamic people of other Middle Eastern countries are not the cruel villains they are often portrayed as being. Fiercely dedicated, yes. Willing to die for what they consider to be a holy cause, without question. But in all the years I spent in Lebanon, in and out of captivity, I don't think I ever met a people more capable of expressing family devotion and simple human kindness than the Lebanese.

Surely there were times when I had been mistreated by a few of them. Some had lost their entire families in the war, and I wondered how I might have reacted if such a tragedy had befallen me.

There had also been moments when I had been shown real concern by some of my captors. Their positions could not have been easy for them. Obviously they had been given orders to treat me as sternly as possible, to allow me no special favors. It had to have been a risk for those who showed me any sympathy, and yet there were a few who did.

The home to which I was taken on September 15, 1991, was immaculately clean. The furniture was nicely arranged, the walls a pleasant pastel color, the marble floors scrubbed. It was a house anyone would have been pleased to live in, and certainly I was, despite my physical condition and the fact that I was still a captive.

The guards were most attentive and followed the doctor's instructions explicitly. Without fail they brought me the food and medication that I needed to recover. And every day they would come in and lift me off the fold-out daybed where I slept. "Time for exercise, Joe," they would say, it seemed to me almost cheerfully. Though I couldn't see their faces, I always imagined there was a smile on their lips as they patiently marched me around the room, one at each side, supporting me by my elbows. "Come, come, Joseph," they would exhort. "Walk. It is important for you."

With their help, it wasn't too long before I was able to move around pretty well. I was fed decently, I was getting the medication I needed, and the pleasant and orderly decor of the place made me feel, sometimes, almost as though I were not a captive any longer.

But the nights were long when I dreamed of Elham and home and freedom. The days were shrouded in semidarkness. The draperies had been arranged so that I was able to see a few shafts of sunlight, though nothing of the outside world. Still, I was able to continue reading and to reach into myself

during hours of meditation, endlessly searching for the strength I needed to survive.

How many times had I read *Jane Eyre,* whose main character had become almost like a distant cousin to me? How many times *Robin Hood,* who had become like a brother in adversity? How often had I pored through the Koran, searching for spiritual help and renewal?

The somewhat simplistic book on mathematics was, in my condition, delightfully fascinating and filled many hours that would otherwise have been lost to me. I have always been intrigued by numbers and, though I don't imagine myself an Einstein, I think I am reasonably skilled in that science. Almost from the first moment of my captivity, I found myself counting the days, the hours—ultimately the months and years. I know the precise date, almost to the hour, of every time I was moved from one location to another. I know the exact number of the sandbags on the rooftop balcony where we were held for one painfully cold winter. And now I decided to recollect the number of times I had read the books that had intimately acquainted me with Jane and Robin, with the message of God as expressed through the Koran.

These may seem like mindless exercises but they kept my intellect alive, my spirits raised. When I had nothing else to stimulate me, other than the prospect of long days in captivity, I looked for anything that would sustain me. What I found amazing was that the answers lay within myself.

My days of recovery were swift. It may be that I got too well too soon, because only a week later I was moved to yet another location. This was only a few miles away, and the usual routine was employed: I was blindfolded, shunted from one car to another. It was a system I had become almost accustomed to, but I still thought it crude and unpleasant. It did, however, allow me a few precious moments to breathe the free air again.

Only after we were in the house and my blindfold was removed did I recognize it. I felt a rush of fear. "Oh, no!" I think I said softly. It was the "Hate House," where the guards had treated me so remorselessly, the house where the "Rifleman" had constantly slapped and kicked and brutalized me for the slightest infraction, or for none at all. I really thought I was in for it. The haven I had just left seemed light years away.

My fears were allayed when I soon discovered that the guards were not people I was able to recognize. Despite my captors' masks, I gained a certain familiarity with them by their voices and, most strikingly, their mannerisms. Then I heard a soft voice that I knew instantly. It was the young guard who had told me of losing his entire family in a tank assault, who held no deep bitterness in his heart, proclaiming it as the will of Allah. How much I admired his courage and his profound faith.

He greeted me warmly, as though we were old friends who had just stumbled on one another. "How are you, Joseph?" he asked. "How are you feeling?" I heard genuine concern in his voice. I knew that he had heard of my recent illness and genuinely cared about my health. How happy I was to meet this young man again. I would be delighted to see him again someday, both of us free men. But of course that would not be possible. If there was one thing all the guards did with diligence, it was to preserve their identities.

Although I was pleased that the "Rifleman" was no longer present at the house, I often wondered if his painfully traumatic wounds had healed and if he had made peace with his God. I would like to think so, but I expect not. His hatred had become so deeply ingrained in him that it is easier for me to picture him as a suicide truck driver ramming a cargo of explosives into an embassy building than someone whose heart has been changed. I believe there are thousands of such bitter and fanatically devoted men and women who remain in the Middle East. I pray that somehow they allow God, who can work miracles, to re-enter their lives.

I was reasonably well-treated at the house during my second stay. The guards' behavior seemed much less hostile than so often in the past. I was still blindfolded some of the time, still in chains that constricted my movements to a narrow part of the room, but I was able to do my daily exercises, to read, to meditate, to hope.

Intuitively I sensed a change, not just because of the guards' treatment of me, or the fact that they even exchanged a few words with me now and then, but because of something indefinable, like a slow, subtle change in the weather. I began to think that the winds of fate were beginning to turn in my favor. It was the soft breeze I had waited and prayed for.

Chapter 16

Elham: It seemed as though the hostages were being released one by one, but still there was no Joseph. I worked hard at trying to keep up with even the smallest turn in the news, anything that might suggest there was some positive change in the negotiations between the Party of God, or Hezbollah, and the Western powers, some turn of events that would lead to Joseph's freedom.

At the same time, my father became seriously ill. He was a generous, kind man, strong but gentle, in many ways like my husband. I think that is why they were so compatible, why they had been able to quickly establish a warm relationship with each other. My father, who had been ill lately, often told me how he prayed for Joseph, how much he wanted to see him alive and free again. "We will have such a good time together," he would say. "I hope I will survive to the day of his freedom, to see him once again." I knew he was pleased with my choice of a husband. If I had been given the choice, I would have been overjoyed with my selection of a father. And now both of them were in serious trouble. My heart was doubly burdened.

As I followed the daily news reports, many things astonished me. The Syrians had actually sided with the Americans in the Gulf War, after twenty years of being bitterly opposed to U.S. influence in the Middle East. They had stood side by side in the desert with the Allied troops to fight off Hussein's army, which they considered to be a far greater threat to their security than anything the West might propose. Hussein, in his attempt to control the oil wealth of the Arab nations, had only succeeded in alienating one of his presumed allies.

When John McCarthy was released late that summer, he brought with him a letter from the kidnappers, which he faithfully delivered to then Secretary-General of the United

Nations, Javier Perez de Cuellar. It was a promising note
that was later discovered to have been written by Sheikh
Muhammad Hussein Fadlallah, the spiritual leader of the
Hezbollah. The note described what the U.N. had to do in
order to resume serious negotiations for the release of the
hostages.

I had met Fadlallah not long after Joseph was taken in
1986. Our meeting had been arranged through an
intermediary, and I was driven to his home in the Dahieh
(south suburb) section of Beirut, where he received me
cordially. He never looked directly at me as I pleaded for
Joseph's freedom. It is forbidden for a sheikh to look directly
into a woman's eyes, as I knew, but I hadn't wanted to meet
his gaze—I had wanted to reach his heart.

I told Sheikh Fadlallah of my husband's dedicated work
at the hospital, how he had worked so hard to help the
suffering people, what a good and kind man he was—a
Muslim like myself, with a faith as great as my own.

The sheikh listened to me patiently, nodding from time
to time, and told me he had no power whatsoever in the
matter. He explained to me that he was the spiritual leader
only, and that I would have to go to the military leader of
the Hezbollah.

Now, five years later, another man entered the picture
who would have a great effect on finally obtaining the release
of Joseph and the other hostages still being held.

His name is Giandomenico Picco, the U.N. Secretary-
General's most trusted aide. Since the end of the Gulf War,
Picco had been working behind the scenes to talk with
diplomats in all the involved Middle Eastern countries, and
with the West as well. He is a tall, quite handsome man
with a quiet but very persuasive manner, who had skillfully
negotiated a cease-fire agreement in the Iran-Iraq war in
1988. As a result, he had gained the confidence of the Iranian
government, something the other hostage negotiators, like
Oliver North and Terry Waite, had tried in vain to do.
Despite all the powerful backing of his own government,
Colonel North had had to return to America to face the
scandal of the Iran-Contra affair. And Waite, who clearly
sought worldwide publicity and "face," had been

contemptuously kidnapped by the very group he had attempted to approach. However sincere their desire to solve the hostage crisis, their efforts were mostly crude and ill-advised.

Picco knew the fate of Terry Waite and how perilous his mission was, and yet he agreed to meet with the various leaders of the kidnap groups. He was never threatened, but later learned that he had come close to being abducted after Israel apparently reneged on a promise to free Shia prisoners who were being held in Israel.

Picco had, as well, to contend with Iranian demands centering around the billions of Iranian dollars that had been frozen in the United States. Many of the demands made by the hostage-takers seemed almost undeliverable, but Picco proceeded to work with a calmness and courage that can only be described as statesmanlike. He traveled constantly from Teheran to Beirut, from Tel Aviv to Damascus, from New York to Washington, never losing hope, never believing that the hostage problem could not be solved, and never fearing for his own safety.

Unlike some others, Picco wasn't seeking self-glorification. Rather, he always tried to remain carefully in the background. But my feeling is that he, more than any other diplomat or government go-between, helped to solve the hostage problem. He did it selflessly, with what I think was real concern and sympathy for the men held captive for so many long and brutal years, regardless of their faith or nationalities. To me, Giandomenico Picco is a true hero. He has said, modestly, that it was only his close relationship with the Iranian government, built up over the years, that made it possible for him to make any progress at all, and that it was the Israelis who almost upset him as he walked a very precarious diplomatic tightrope. Their major concern was in learning the fate of missing Israeli prisoners. Without that, it seemed they had little interest in the fate of other Western hostages. But Picco continued to work for all captives, regardless of their country. He felt that the hostage situation had gone on far too long, that neither side had anything to gain by keeping innocent men in chains—and he was able to convince Rafsanjani of this.

The Iranian president offered the Hezbollah leaders arms worth millions of dollars in exchange for each hostage released. I knew none of this, of course. Picco was working in absolute secrecy; even his colleagues at the United Nations were unaware of his activities. But slowly, one by one, the hostages were being released.

First, there was the former British war hero, Jackie Mann. He had been a Spitfire pilot in World War II and had been shot down six times. After the war he had become a commercial pilot for Middle East Airlines, a Lebanese carrier. After he retired he opened a place called the Pickwick Bar, but the Islamic Jihad blew it up because they objected to the sale of liquor. Jackie Mann was in his seventies when he was abducted, and spent almost three years in captivity.

That was in September. The next month Jesse Turner, a teacher at the Beirut University College, was let go. Picco said his freedom was obtained at a very heavy cost, undoubtedly in armaments from the Iranian government, which had gotten them through the United States in the first place. Picco has said that other hostages were released without any payment.

In November, Thomas Sutherland, who had been the dean of agriculture at the American University and a friend of Joseph's, was freed. I had been in almost daily contact with his wife, Jean, who had remained at the American University during Thomas's captivity. Together, we had exhausted every effort to obtain our husbands' freedom. Thomas had been taken at a time when the kidnapping of Americans was increasing, and he had been held for over six years. I was thrilled to hear of his release and was so happy for Jean.

That same month, Terry Waite was released by the Islamic Jihad. His release was deliberately delayed by the terrorists, who felt that Waite had betrayed them. They had told him not to return to Lebanon, but he had done so anyway. Now they didn't want it to appear that Waite had had anything to do with the release of any hostage. Still, Waite held a twenty-minute press conference after his release, in which he suggested it was he, and not Giandomenico Picco, who had ultimately secured the freedom of the hostages. How he could have done this—since he had been taken captive in January of 1987—is a mystery. But Waite appears to be a vain man looking for self-glorification more than anything else. He even insisted on having his beard trimmed twice, claiming that he couldn't face his public looking as he did.

I kept waiting for news of Joseph. Why was he being held for so long, when so many others were being released?

My dear father died that fall before realizing his deep wish to see Joseph a free man once again. Joseph's sister, Rose, had also passed away. His oldest son, Joseph, had succumbed to a massive heart attack. Now his father-in-law was also gone. My husband would have to face some very difficult moments even after he was released, and I still had no assurance that that would ever happen.

My mind was filled, day and night, with every kind of scenario, but in my calmest moments I always knew that Joseph would work his way through any difficulty he might confront in captivity. He was a very determined man and had a strong faith in God. But each passing day was an eternity.

I continued to pray.

Chapter 17

Joseph: I was still kept ignorant of any progress in the hostage situation, but for some reason that I cannot quite explain, my confidence was growing. I had survived the strange operation and my health improved almost daily. I became stronger, able to resume my exercises without pain or discomfort. The guards were civil, but there were times when I saw them looking at me oddly. I couldn't see their faces, of course, but I was able to detect a certain change in their manner. It gave me the feeling that they knew of events of which I was kept completely ignorant.

If I had been aware of how skillfully Giandomenico Picco had been working on behalf of all the hostages, I might have burst into song, or at least a rousing cheer. But it had been so long since I had been abducted, and there were times when it was difficult to fight off the feeling that I had been abandoned and forgotten by the outside world. On those occasions I would remember Jean-Louis Normandin and his warning never to allow myself to fall into a mire of self-pity and despair. There were moments when I could almost hear his soft but firm voice of encouragement. "Don't let them defeat you, Joseph. They have only taken your body, don't let them take your soul and your spirit."

He wasn't referring to the guards, who were only minions of the terrorist hierarchy. I learned that the guards were paid in U.S. dollars, about $300 to $500 a month. In many ways they were as much captive as we were, all of us pawns in a political war of which very few of us could make any sense. I have the feeling that many of them yearned to return to their families as eagerly as we did, however uncertain it would make their economic future.

I even began to think of how fortunate I was, compared to many others who had been taken hostage. I knew that some had died in captivity, some had been executed. And one, Edward Tracy, had almost no one to turn to. He had led such a peripatetic life, wandering from one city to another in Europe and the Middle East, that he seemed never to have made any close attachments. He was truly a rolling stone. I wonder if this didn't have something to do with his eventual mental breakdown. There is no question that he might have been helped in the early stages of his illness, but having been taken hostage must have made his condition worse. In the more than four years that I was chained with Tracy, I think I developed a true compassion for the plight of innocent people, and I begged God for Edward's deliverance. I continue to do so.

How fortunate I was! I had Elham, whose name literally means "inspiration" in English. I was certain that she was doing everything possible to gain my freedom. I had my family in America, my sons, my daughter, my brother Tom, my sisters, Rose and Helen. I was totally convinced that all of my family and many of my close friends hadn't forgotten me. That conviction helped to take me through many a dark and lonely night. At times, it made me feel almost invincible.

On November 4, 1991, I was unexpectedly moved to another location. It was a great improvement over the "Hate House," where the walls had been blackened over with what I suspect had been a stove fire, leaving a lingering stench in the air.

In this new place, which I believe was also in Sidon—the South of Lebanon area where many hostages were held—I was led into a kitchen that had virtually no fixtures, as though it had been abandoned long before. I came to think of it as the "Tombstone House."

Previously, I had been chained to radiators, to sink pipes, to iron rods that had been drilled and fitted into the floor. Here I was propped into a corner of the kitchen, where my leg was manacled to a steel link attached to a heavy block of concrete. It was the shortest chain I had been tethered to in all my years of captivity.

But I remained quiet and complaisant. I couldn't exercise as freely as I would have liked because my movements were so constricted, snubbed down to a chain no more than a few inches long. I was still able to read, though, and to meditate. Now that I was alone, more or less in solitary confinement and without Edward's incessant distractions, I was able to reach even more deeply into myself.

If there is one thing I learned and came to believe more fervently than ever, it is the lesson of forgiveness. It was, for me, an almost miraculous perception.

Surely there had been moments when I despised my captors for the precious years they had stolen from me, abducting me at a time when my life with Elham was so wonderful, when my work at the university and at the hospital made me feel that I was a more caring and productive member of society than at any other moment in my life. But I came to feel that by condemning my captors I was only condemning myself. "Don't get mad, get even," is a somewhat popular notion. I came to a loftier conclusion, a message taught by all the great religions since the beginning of man: that love is a far more powerful weapon than hate. If I were set free, I would not want to come out a hateful and embittered man.

These thoughts may have been in my mind when, on November 25th, 1991, the guards came into the kitchen and unchained me. "Come with us, Joseph," one of them said. "We are going to another place." I took one last look at the concrete block to which I had been chained for two weeks, happy to be rid of that constant reminder of my own mortality. Then I stood patiently as they blindfolded me and led me out of the house.

The night air of the Lebanese countryside was pure and refreshing after so many days in the squalid kitchen. I breathed it in hungrily and felt I could almost smell the fragrance of blossoming flowers. I remembered my resolve to take Elham to the Rose Bowl Parade in Pasadena, which may seem trite but which had become a symbol of renewal, of freedom, of the life we would share again someday. If I were ever released.

In all of the many times I was moved from one location to another, I had the agonizing thought that I might be taken to some desolate area in Lebanon and quickly executed.

It was difficult for me not to remember the sad, contorted expression on the face of my friend Peter Kilburn, as he lay in the morgue of the University Medical Center. I had always felt that I might have to confront a similar fate. There were times when I felt almost resigned to it.

Once more I was crammed into the trunk of the first car, smelling once more what had become almost familiar fragrances: the upholstery, the car exhaust. But again I retreated into silence and wondering. God, how grateful I am that I wasn't claustrophobic!

I would hear the car stop and the trunk lid opened, and feel strong hands and arms lifting me out and carrying me to another car. I might hear a few muttered words in Arabic, but the guards had very little difficulty with me. By this time I weighed only a little more than 130 pounds. I was moved three times this way on a trip that seemed interminable but took no more than about one hour. I had the distinct feeling that we were driving back to Beirut, and I proved to be right.

We finally reached our destination and I was put into a room that was sparsely furnished but, to my amazement, had wall-to-wall carpeting. I thought it must be the home of a high official in the Hezbollah.

I was also surprised to discover that some of the guards who had been with me at the previous location were still with me. Usually, the contingent changed from one site to another and I always wondered, sometimes with trepidation, how the new group would treat me. But I had the strong feeling that something was up, that a decision had been made somewhere. What it was I had no way of knowing.

Then another surprise. My chains were removed! I had been manacled at the wrist or ankle since February 1987, and having the chains off gave me a sense of freedom I hadn't experienced for so very long. I was able to move around a lot more easily, almost as if I were back in the real world, although I was still restricted to the pad on which I slept.

Another blessing was that I was not blindfolded so frequently, although whenever the guards were about to enter my room, I was ordered to face the wall and stay in a fixed position until they had left.

We exchanged very few words, but once again I sensed that something unusual was happening. I suspect that the guards knew that I was going to be released at last, and that they wanted to share the good news with me. But, of course, they were not allowed to give me any information.

My hopes had risen, but there had been so many, many disappointments over the years that I refused to allow myself the luxury of thinking that I might be released at last. Normandin's counseling once again entered my mind. "Don't ever believe anything the guards tell you," he had said repeatedly. By this time I had learned to strengthen the resolve I had to survive every day of my captivity. Not to think of tomorrow but to live, as well as possible, for each moment. When one of the guards whispered to me, "Things are going well for you," I only smiled at him and thought, "I'll believe that when it happens."

The thought of gaining my freedom was almost unbearable. If I were to raise my hopes only to be denied again, I don't know how I would survive. Better not to expect what I had hoped and prayed for. Much wiser to anticipate the worst and to ready myself for it. In some ways I was preparing as much for the end of my life as I was for a new beginning. As I had many times during my captivity, I thought of how I would face my execution. I hoped bravely and without fear, with the understanding that the young Arab boy had taught me, that it was "the will of Allah."

I was looking forward to another bleak Christmas in confinement when the guards came into my room with an exchange of clothing. "Get dressed, Joseph," they said. "You're going home."

I had heard those words before only to be turned back, and so I refused to actually believe that this was the moment I had so desperately looked forward to for more than five years. But then I was handed a pair of shoes, the first I had worn in all that time. Slacks, a shirt, a sweater. Could this be the real thing? Again, I refused to raise my hopes too high, yet it was difficult to repress my enthusiasm. I was as excited as a schoolboy going to his graduation.

After I was washed and dressed, feeling somewhat

awkward in what I hoped were my "freedom clothes," the guards led me into the living room. I might have stumbled in my new shoes. They seemed so strange after having worn sandals or no footwear at all for such a long time.

There was a cardboard box waiting for me there, the kind you might deliver a large home appliance in. One of the guards told me to get into the box, which I did without any protest. Apparently I was to be the appliance. But I still had no firm assurance that I was going home rather than being driven to some remote spot and pistol shot, or taken to the end of a long pier and unceremoniously dumped into the waters of Beirut Harbor. All kinds of possibilities entered my mind.

I tried to prepare myself for the worst as well as the best.

Chapter 18

Elham: I first learned that Joseph was about to be released from a newspaper report in the independent Beirut newspaper, *An-Nahar*. The Revolutionary Justice Organization released a report to them and to the Western media that he would be released that day. They said:

> "The Revolutionary Justice Organization announces that it will free the American Joseph Cicippio within the 24 hours coming."

The message went on to say that the RJO had received reassuring messages from the United Nations about releasing Arab prisoners in Israel, in Europe, and in what Israel described as its "security zone" in southern Lebanon. Those detainees numbered in the hundreds.

My heart leapt at the thought that Joseph might at last be free again. At the same time, it was tinged with sadness that Joseph's son, and his sister, Rose, had not lived to see this day. And I was still mourning the death of my father, Najib, whose name means "proud" in English. How prideful he would have been to embrace his son-in-law again, to see him and welcome him. He had spoken so many times of it.

In the midst of my excitement, I wondered, another cruel disappointment? Ambassador Crocker called me and asked me to prepare myself. I heard in his voice that he was withholding confirmation and high hopes this time, although it was the same tender, soft voice with whom I had built a very nice relationship. On many occasions, I felt he was living my tragedy and sharing my worries. I can say that he was one of the few politicians who was very sensitive and held true feelings. He was a rare, kind ambassador, very sharp, a real diplomat, and strong but with a soft heart. I have great respect for him. We agreed to keep in contact. He called back, saying, "We are going to send a car to bring you to the embassy to watch the news closely."

I spent the whole evening packing. All my neighbors, friends, part of my family who had heard the great news, came to see me. I was very happy, but afraid that there would be another disappointment.

The next morning, as scheduled, the embassy car met me at 10:00 a.m. and drove me, along with my mother, to the embassy in Aukar in East Beirut. On our way I started hearing the walkie-talkies asking from the embassy how far we were. My heart started pounding and I knew for sure that something positive had happened. The driver started driving faster, and the air was filled with tension. When we finally reached the embassy, we were greeted by the ambassador and his wife. He was holding a large bouquet of flowers, which he presented to me, and with his soft, tender voice, he said, "Joseph has been released."

His eyes were shining with tears of joy. He understood the suffering we had endured for so many years. I think I have never met a kinder, more sympathetic government official than Ambassador Crocker, and silently I thanked God for allowing us his support and friendship.

"I have arranged a motor escort to drive you and your mother to Damascus," he said. "You will meet Joseph there."

We were led to two cars and began the journey to the Syrian capital. I was almost overcome with the anticipation of seeing Joseph again after such a long and painful time. As swiftly as the driver went, it was not fast enough for me. But then, when we reached the outskirts of the city, we found the border clogged with traffic and people. It was election day in Syria, and everyone who was outside the country was obliged to return and vote and then to celebrate the victor, even if there was only one candidate.

When a man paused and put his hand on the hood of our slowly moving vehicle as he crossed the street, I felt a momentary flash of anger. But then I realized that these people had no idea of who we were or how urgent our journey was. It was their holiday, after all, as important to them as a 4th of July celebration in an American town or city. I sat back and decided to be patient. I had waited for so many years, and I had more reason to be joyous than any of many years, and I had more reason to be joyous than any of them. My moment would come.

Another car accompanied us to secure our trip and take us safely through any checkpoints we would meet. At the Syrian border, we were switched to another U.S. government car, which came from the U.S. Embassy in Syria to bring us safely to the home of the U.S. charge d'affaires.

Chapter 19

Joseph: I felt kind of absurd when I crawled into the box and curled up into as comfortable a position as I could find. I thought, Well, what now? They've done just about everything else to me. Maybe I'm going to be delivered this way, in a kind of mock ceremony.

Holes had been punched in the cardboard, so at least I could breathe. I thought that was a good sign, but then wondered if it was meant to allow the water to rush inside the box after they had dumped my body in the river.

I would not allow myself to think that after more than five years my captors were finally going to release me from bondage. Maybe my death would be a fitting way to end my captivity, to complete the agony of so many endless days and nights. To see Elham again, and my family, simply transcended anything I could permit myself to imagine.

After the box was sealed, I was raised aloft. I could hear the guards muttering as they struggled with me down the narrow staircase and then out to the trunk of yet another automobile. I cautioned myself to remain quiet and uncomplaining.

Again I was moved from car to car. After the third exchange I was removed from the carton and put, blindfolded, into the rear seat of an automobile. I sensed that we were on a country lane, in a wooded area somewhere. I thought, is this my final destination? Would I be led out now into the trees, to be shot and left to be found, perhaps weeks later?

I heard the car engine silenced and the opening of doors. There were brief exchanges in Arabic spoken by my captors and I wondered what orders were being given. Take him into the woods? Shoot him? Let's get out of here? I had no idea what they were saying.

Then a voice said, "I am going to remove your blindfold. Keep your eyes tightly shut. We are going to be very close nearby, and if you do anything foolish we will take you back with us, or we will kill you."

I sat trying not to move a muscle, keeping my eyes sealed, still wondering if a bullet wasn't about to come crashing into my brain. Probably only seconds passed before I heard another car approach and its engine turned off.

There were the sounds of steps approaching me on the rough, graveled road and then another voice spoke from an opened window at my side.

"Are you Joseph Cicippio?" the man asked.

I sat there frozen in fear until the voice said, in a kindly but almost business-like way, "You can open your eyes now. You are on your way back to freedom."

He helped me to stumble from the car and told me that he was a representative of the Syrian government and that now I was in their hands. "You are safe," he assured me. "Your troubles are behind you."

Still I could not shake the idea that this was some elaborate plot, that I might even have been traded from one group of hostage-takers to another. It was hard for me to believe that my day of deliverance had arrived at last.

However, I was reassured to notice that none of the four men who accompanied me was masked. If they were terrorists or another team of hired guards, they would surely not have wished to reveal their identities, unless they had planned to leave me lifeless on some remote highway. I found it difficult not to entertain these macabre ideas.

It was a long ride to Damascus, one that would normally take about two hours or so. I was impatient, of course, still disbelieving that I might actually be free after so many years. But I gloried in the view of the countryside, the lush, verdant woods, the clear blue sky. It had been so long.

And the people! When we reached the outskirts of Damascus, the roads were crowded with them. I tried to look into each face, to remember what an unmasked, unthreatening human being looked like. I saw joy in all of them, friendliness and love, a universal happiness beyond anything I had ever imagined. They were free.

When I asked one of the men why so many people were in the streets, he explained that it was election day in Damascus. "Everyone must come out," he said. "It is a national show of support for our government." And then he added, "I know you are anxious to reach your family, Cicippio, but you must be patient." How could I argue? I thought I might soon experience the greatest celebration of my life.

We reached the Syrian government house late in the afternoon of December 2. My Syrian drivers wished me well and quickly departed. Then I was led up the stairs and ushered into the office of a high Syrian official who was obviously familiar with all the negotiations that had taken place.

He greeted me with a kind of reserved enthusiasm, then stepped back and looked at me head to toe.

"No," he said. "It will not do. Today is a national holiday in Syria and you must be dressed accordingly." He picked up his inter-office phone and spoke a few words, and an aide promptly entered the office.

The official spoke a few more words, and before long the aide returned with a complete change of wardrobe: a suit, shirt, ties, socks, everything I needed to look like a proper gentleman.

When I looked at myself in the mirror, I was unable to recognize the man who had been abducted more than five years earlier. I was more than sixty pounds lighter, my face had taken on a gray pallor, the new suit I wore seemed to hang on my shoulders. I was also a different person in other ways, and I hoped that Elham would accept me. A small, reassuring voice told me that she would. I had always felt that our love for each other, and our faith, could surmount any difficulty no matter how great.

When the Syrian emissary decided that I was suitably dressed, he nodded approvingly. "All right," he said. "Now we will take you to the American Embassy."

"Is my wife there?" I asked anxiously. "Is Elham there?"

A small smile crossed his lips. "I suspect she is," he said reassuringly.

I prayed that at last I would be reunited with Elham.

How long it had been.

Chapter 20

Elham: After waiting for almost two hours at the home of the charge d'affaires, we were offered lunch. It was very thoughtful of his wife, but we couldn't eat. Finally, the telephone rang, and we got the green signal to move to the American Embassy.

I can clearly remember the endless traffic lights on our way, which wasn't usual in Lebanon, because some of them had been stolen and others weren't functioning anymore. We finally arrived at the embassy's entrance, went through the security gate, passed the guards, and reached the main building. They opened the door and I looked inside the large room. I think I recall a large, crystal chandelier hanging from the ceiling. "Tell me, is Joseph here?" Something in the broad smiles on their faces told me that he was. It was as if they were sharing my excitement, my happiness.

"Joseph has just finished a press conference with the Syrian prime minister, the U.S. ambassador, and the U.N. delegation, and is waiting for you," one of them replied.

The room was so huge I couldn't find Joseph at first. Then, in a corner of the room, I saw what I thought was a small boy, sitting on the edge of his chair. I didn't realize that it was Joseph until he made a fast move, stood up, and walked towards me.

"Joseph?" I said.

"Elham! I can't believe my eyes," he said as we embraced. For long moments we wept, holding each other, unable to speak.

This was the moment I had prayed for, that had been in my dreams every night for five years. Then he looked beside me and saw my mother, and in a very tender way, he said, "Mama, it's so good you are here. Where is your father, Elham?" I didn't want to give him the bad news at this first moment, but the recent grievance of my father's death was

too obvious to hide. We all cried when he realized that my
father had passed away only two months ago.

I tried to act as cheerfully as I could, but I was distraught

at how thin and frail he had become. But when I looked
into his eyes, I saw the fire and spirit there. I had worried all
those years how his captivity would affect him—how he
was going to survive. Now I knew and thanked God that he
had come back whole and intact. He was like a diamond in
the dust. All you have to do is blow the dust off for it to
shine again.

We sat together for long moments quietly talking to each
other, our hands entwined as though we never wanted them
to be separated again. The ambassador announced that a
U.S. military airplane was waiting at the airport and that we

should leave the embassy, but first appear before the press, where hundreds were waiting in the embassy garden. One of the press people kindly asked me, "Mrs. Cicippio, kiss your husband." I simply refused to obey them anymore, and felt relieved. I tried to remain as much in the background as I could. This was Joseph's moment in the sun.

I was amazed to discover how little bitterness there was in Joseph's heart. He spoke in a steady voice, facing an army of cameramen and journalists.

There were still hostages being held and Joseph repeated much of what he had said on a videotape just before his release.

"The Revolutionary Justice Organization has been good to me and cared for me very well during the period of time that I have been with them, and have always tended to my needs in a humanitarian way."

One look at his thin, haggard face would discourage anyone from believing that statement but, amazingly, he reentered the free world determined not to hold any bitterness or hatred for his captors, even those who had treated him most cruelly.

"What good would it do, Elham?" he said to me. "It wouldn't change anything. All it could possibly do is to make me an angry person." The purity of his heart, the lightness of his spirit, is what impressed me most about this "new" Joseph. But then he had always been a gentle and forgiving man. He was really the same Joseph I had known five years before. The same man I will always love and admire so profoundly.

Chapter 21

Joseph: When I reached the American Embassy, I was greeted by Ambassador Ross. The questions began to flow almost instantly, of course, but I was almost too excited to concentrate, knowing that in a few moments I would see Elham again.

She tells me that she thought I was a little boy sitting there on the edge of my seat, and that's exactly how I felt: like a small boy at Christmastime waiting to open his presents. I was so excited I could hardly sit up straight.

What a wonderful moment it was when I saw her start across the floor. I met her halfway there and we just held each other. Except to speak her name, I was unable to say anything. My joy was indescribable. This was simply the greatest moment of my life and I could almost have thanked my captors for allowing me this fantastic experience.

The officials let us have a few private moments together which we spent more or less just gazing at each other. I had never stopped loving Elham, but now I was smitten all over again.

But then those precious minutes passed, too swiftly for me, and I was told that there was a press conference waiting, where the U.N. official, Giandomenico Picco, would be present. I was pleased, because I wanted to personally thank him for his efforts on behalf of the hostages. More than any other man I think he was the most skillful and dedicated in working to free us.

Picco had become somewhat disillusioned by the political in-fighting at the United Nations and resigned his post the following summer, but not until every last hostage was released, including two Germans who were held until June 1992. He was also effective in obtaining the bodies of those hostages who had died in captivity.

A short while after the press conference, Elham and I

were asked to prepare for a trip to Germany. We were to be flown to the Rhein-Main air base outside Frankfurt and then were to go on to the American military hospital in nearby Wiesbaden, where I would undergo a State Department debriefing as well as a thorough medical examination.

I was all eagerness, happy at that moment to get as far away from the Middle East as possible. I love the land and the people there, but I suppose I was going through a sort of post-traumatic experience. After five painful years in captivity, I wanted to be in some safe haven where I could feel free and unthreatened. It wasn't until the wheels of the plane were off the ground and we were in the air, that I felt safe.

We were accompanied by several officials who represented various departments of the U.S. government; I imagine the CIA, the FBI, the Justice Department, the Department of Defense, the State Department, and so forth, but I never really knew who represented which bureau. They interrogated me relentlessly whenever they had the opportunity: at the airport when we were waiting to board the plane, on the plane itself, at the base in Rhein-Main, and even at the medical facility in Wiesbaden. Whenever I came out of an examining room, there was always the debriefing team waiting for me. It made me feel, at times, as though I were the malefactor.

The British hostages were treated very differently. They were introduced to a psychological debriefing program that would help them make an easier adjustment to society. I'm not sure how much such a program would have benefited me, because I had already begun my own psychological evaluation years before, in the early days of my captivity, and had been able to renew it under the strong encouragement of Jean-Louis Normandin while we were prisoners together. In many ways, I came out a more whole man than I had been when first taken hostage. I felt I had captured the strength to endure almost any indignity.

Those first hours of the day when I was finally released had left me almost giddy with happiness. Only the night before I had been held in the dark confines of a lonely and desolate prison room, not knowing what my future was. Now I had smelled the fresh, clean air of freedom. I had seen a beautiful azure sky, then the soft, twilit night of Damascus as we sped toward the airport. Most exhilarating of all, I had Elham beside me.

As the plane took off, with Elham clutching my hand, I could barely restrain my happiness. I joked and kidded with the State Department men who accompanied us, but they rarely relaxed their serious official demeanor.

Then a flight attendant approached our seats, and looked down at me with sadness, a brave smile playing around her lips, her soft, brown eyes moist. If she had known how elated I was at that moment she might have smiled more broadly. I wasn't in the best shape of my life, I only weighed 132 pounds, and all the excitement of the day had tired me somewhat. But I had survived in mind and spirit, and most importantly I was free and on the first leg of my journey home.

In a quietly solicitous voice, the flight attendant asked, "Is there anything special you would like for dinner, Mr. Cicippio?"

I tried to lighten the mood and said as enthusiastically as I could, "I'll have anything as long as it's good and hot." It had been so long since I'd had a hot meal that I'd almost forgotten what one tasted like.

"How about coq au vin?" she said, a bit more brightly now.

"Chicken? Wow!" I said. "That sounds great."

And it was, beautifully prepared and presented. For a brief moment I remembered the first meal I had been served in captivity, on TWA dishes and silverware, but then I tried to shake it from my mind. I didn't want anything to spoil this moment. But, intuitively I felt that there was something I didn't know, something that Elham had been holding back from me.

Chapter 22

Elham: On the plane, Joseph asked me to tell him what had happened while he had been a hostage. For five years he had heard nothing of his family or anything else of the outside world.

"Tell me the good news and the bad news," he said, "the bad news first."

I had been waiting for what I thought might be the right moment to tell him, when we were alone and he could grieve in private. But I knew the moment had arrived; I couldn't hold back any longer. I wanted very much to tell him the sad news myself and took his hand.

"Joseph, you must be strong. Your sister Rose died of cancer. She fought very hard to live long enough to see you again, but it was too much for her."

His face darkened and he slumped forward in his seat. I put my arm consolingly around his shoulders. "There is something else, Joe, that I have to tell you." I felt his body stiffen and he nodded his head quickly.

I spoke as softly as I could. "Your son, Joseph, died of a heart attack."

Now he simply broke down. He drew his breath in sharply and sobbed. He wept bitterly. He had suffered for so long and now, in the first hours of his freedom, he had to hear this terrible news. Joseph, Jr., was his first-born, only thirty-six years old, and had worked so hard fighting for his father's release. I think the effort was simply too much for him.

After long moments, Joseph sighed and dried his tears. Then he looked around as if he were hoping that no one had seen him break down. He turned to me and gazed into my eyes. I could see the strength and courage in his expression. "I'm all right," he said quietly.

Then I told him that my father, Najib Gandhour, had passed away two months before Joseph's release. I wanted

him to know everything, not to be told suddenly and
unexpectedly. We sat silently for a long while, sharing each
other's grief, our hands clasped tightly.

"They wanted so much to see you free again, Joseph," I
told him. "My father spoke of nothing else. And Joseph
worked so hard for you."

"Yes, I know," he said sadly. "I wanted to see them again,
too. They were in my thoughts every day. Sometimes I even
dreamt about seeing us all together again."

My poor Joseph, I thought, what terrible loneliness he
had endured.

Chapter 23

Joseph: When we got to Rhein-Main air base I felt kind of whipped and, of course, deeply saddened by the news Elham had given me. The State Department men didn't wait to begin questioning me again. They explained that knowing all the details of my abduction and captivity would help them to deal more effectively with future hostage situations. I was tempted to say, "You mean the way you did with me?" But that would have been too cynical, and

might have even disrupted the inner peace I had gained after so long and painful an experience.

I'm human, after all, and will certainly feel anger rising within me again. But at least I feel that I have found the means to fight if off. Anger and hatred are emotions that are simply too enervating.

I'm reminded of the story of the priest who is admonishing some young ruffians in his parish. "It takes twice as many facial muscles to frown as it does to smile, so why be angry?" he says. He beams at them, thinking he has won them over until one young cynic replies, "More exercise!" It's kind of a funny story, but my sentiments are with the parish priest.

But the State Department men were only doing their jobs and, as tired as I was, I answered their questions as patiently as I could. I would do so many times in the months to come. And if any information I was able to give them would help avoid a hostage crisis in the future, or alleviate one should it arise, I was more than eager to cooperate.

Finally, our transportation arrived to take us to the medical center, only a short distance away. When we got there we saw blue and white balloons decorating the railing and a huge sign over the front entrance that read: "Welcome Home, Mr. Cicippio." I was stunned. It was after 11:00 p.m. on a very cold night, the temperature was just around freezing— but there were several hundred people out there to greet us.

Many of them called out to me, told me how happy they were that I was free, and gave me encouraging pats on the back. A few asked how I was feeling, but even though I was exhausted and full of sadness from the news about our family, I tried to manage a brave smile. "Tonight I feel terrific," I told them, even though I didn't quite feel that way.

I thanked them all for coming out so late at night in such cold weather, and then we entered the medical center. After a midnight snack of sandwiches I was directed to a very clean and pleasant hospital suite, in stark contrast to the bleak and verminous conditions I had been held in for so long. It was hard to believe that only the night before I had slept in dismal confinement, not really certain of my future. My captors had told me four days earlier that I would be released and to prepare myself for it, but I stubbornly refused to believe them until it actually happened. Even now I almost felt as though it was all a dream. I had to pinch myself to believe I was actually free again.

There were times in captivity when I had thought of myself as the most forgotten man in the universe, but already I'd been treated with great warmth and kindness and that would continue in a way I could not possibly have imagined. I learned that people the world over are greatly concerned about even a single human life, even of someone totally unknown to them. With this thought I drifted off into a soft and pleasant sleep.

They allowed me to have a long rest, for which I was very grateful. Just being able to go to the bathroom whenever I wished, without a hooded guard standing just inside or outside the door and urging me to hurry, was a great luxury. It occurred to me more than once that those things that we take for granted in our daily lives are often the most important.

Then I got wonderful news. Alann Steen, a teacher at the Beirut University College, had been released by his captors the day after I was. He had been kidnapped along with three other BUC academics—Jesse Turner, Robert Polhill, and Mitheleshwar Singh—but had been held longer than any of them for no reason anyone could figure out.

Alann had been particularly brutalized in captivity. Once, when he had innocently prolonged an exercise program, a guard had beaten him mercilessly, smashing his head against a wall. I learned later that he would need medical treatment for the rest of his life, since his brain had been permanently damaged in the assault. I am pleased and encouraged to hear that he has made great progress despite the seizures he occasionally experiences.

Now, I thought, there was only one American hostage left—Terry Anderson, who was the Middle East bureau chief of the Associated Press. I prayed for him. The next day my prayers were answered when he, too, was released after spending almost seven years in captivity, longer than any of us. Once again, who could understand why the Islamic Jihad for the Liberation of Palestine had held him for so long?

Unless it was because he was an outspoken journalist who reported conditions the way he saw them. In the Middle East, the newspapers are largely government-controlled and they expect outside writers to adhere to whatever opinion the party line or the underground factions dictate.

I'm not sure I would agree with every conclusion that Terry Anderson made in those difficult years, but I would never have prevented him from saying what I believe he honestly felt. He wasn't shouting "Fire!" in a crowded theater in order to alarm the people. He was, in a brave and conscientious way, trying to alert them to the fact that the building was already ablaze. Right or wrong, whatever he wrote was honest, but it had cost him almost seven years of his life.

The news of every hostage's release was very consoling to me. I tried to imagine how difficult their lives had been in captivity, and though I had never actually seen any of them, with the exception of Edward Tracy and Jean-Louis Normandin, I could hear their voices through the walls of a few places where we were briefly held together and tried to imagine who they were. But I had never been allowed to meet with them. For most of the time I spent in captivity, my confinement was often solitary, with my ankles chained only a few feet apart.

In a sense, the fact that I couldn't rely on anyone else had been my salvation. Other than the inspiration that Normandin provided during the nine months we were held together, I had no way to turn except to look within myself for the spiritual strength I needed to survive.

Chapter 24

Elham: Our reception at Wiesbaden was wonderful. I was treated so cordially and with such warmth and kindness that I thought I was the returning hostage instead of Joseph.

I knew we would be separated most of the time for the next few days while he underwent medical examinations, but I was happy that at last he was in the friendly hands of people who cared only about his well-being.

I was taken to another building at the medical center where I would spend the next few days. I was overwhelmed by the luxurious suite they brought me to, as splendid as anything I might have imagined in the world's finest hotels. And I was treated almost as if I were royalty.

For the first day, they tried to keep me as occupied as possible. Two of the United States staff and a Red Cross representative drove me to a shop to choose a wardrobe for Joseph composed of quite a few necessities: underwear, shoes, socks, shirts—even a suit. The clothing was provided by the Red Cross. Although I had brought a suitcase with me filled with Joseph's clothes, I had not thought that he wouldn't be able to wear them. All those years I had been watching the hostages who were released before him… I had kept a suitcase ready for Joseph, because I wanted to see him just as he had been before.

When I returned to the hospital I was given exciting news. Joseph's brother Thomas, with his lovely wife Frances and two of Joseph's sons, David and Eric, were flying to Wiesbaden for what I knew would be a wonderful family reunion. I only wished that Joseph's sister, Helen Fazio, could have been with them, but she was desperately ill and unable to travel.

I thought of how faithful and loving Joseph's family had been throughout all of his ordeal. All of them had been willing to make almost any sacrifice to see Joseph free again.

Helen, even in her weakened condition, had found the strength to write a plea to the terrorists begging them to release her brother. It was never answered. Five months before Joseph's release she had been given two months to live, but she had stubbornly and bravely hung on, waiting for the day when she could embrace him again.

All his sons—Joseph, Jr., Richard, David, Paul, Eric, and Allan—had worked tirelessly on Joseph's behalf. His daughter, Beth Ann, his nieces, Helen Melnick and Judi Suita, his brothers—everyone in his family had worked and prayed for Joseph's return.

I believe that was the answer. I read later that when the family was assembled at the airport in Philadelphia, waiting to fly to Wiesbaden, a young soldier on leave from Kuwait on his way home to his family in New York said, "That's the hostage's family. Boy, how did that guy survive?"

How does anyone survive what seems almost unbearable? I share Joseph's belief that through steadfast faith and prayer there is nothing we cannot overcome, no matter what God we appeal to. We are all tested at some time in our lives. Joseph's trial was particularly severe but he never surrendered his faith, never lost his love for people.

All of us had lived through a painful nightmare. But we had never given up hope. I think that our fervent prayers and the prayers of millions of people around the world who felt great sympathy for the innocent hostages had a great deal to do with Joseph's ultimate freedom.

Chapter 25

Joseph: For the few days I was at Wiesbaden I was checked from head to toe, to the point that I almost began to feel like a laboratory animal! But I was grateful to be given such thorough and devoted attention. I was a free man, after all, in a hospital run by the American government. And no one wore a mask to conceal their identity or taped my eyes so I couldn't see.

I saw only smiling faces as I went from one examination room to another. "How are you feeling, Joe?" they would ask, and offer encouraging remarks like, "You're in great shape, Mister Cicippio. The EKG, the CAT Scan, they all look very good."

One of the doctors said, "Everything's coming up roses. You'll be going home soon."

Roses. I remembered again how I had dreamt of roses while I was a captive and had resolved to take Elham to Pasadena for the Rose Bowl Parade when I got home. But first I was eager to see my family again.

One of the things that mystified my doctors was the reason for the operation that had been performed on me in Beirut. They actually had a few lively arguments about what the cause could have been, and asked me over and over what my symptoms were. I told them: intense abdominal pain, nausea, fever, the inability to even stand and walk. They examined the incision over and over while they questioned me.

One doctor said: "Well, they did a very nice job."

"Yes," I replied. "They were very gentle. Very concerned. The surgeon who actually did the operation was particularly kind. When I felt him probing my body his hands were like the touch of God."

"Well, maybe it was God," the doctor said, smiling. I grinned back at him. "In any case he was a very skillful surgeon."

Another asked, "Didn't they ever tell you the reason for your condition?"

I shook my head. "I wanted to know and asked him but he never responded. It was for the same reason that my eyes were taped. My captors didn't want me to be able to identify them, and that was encouraging in a way. I thought it meant that they might release me someday. If I couldn't identify them they were free and clear once they let me go."

One doctor was incredulous. "You mean that in over five years you never saw the face of a single guard?"

"No. Their security was very tight, very professional. I think that was the reason they never allowed me to read a newspaper or to hear a radio broadcast or even to glimpse the surroundings outside of the rooms I was held in. The less I knew, the safer they felt."

Always, after each examination, one or two of the ubiquitous State Department men were waiting to ply me with further questions.

I told them the exact date, almost to the hour, of each time I was moved; the method by which we were transported, the blindfolds, the car trunks in which we lay, the areas in and around Beirut where I thought we had been taken. Much of this information couldn't have been new to them; other hostages had been treated in much the same way.

One of them—CIA, FBI, Justice Department, by that time I could hardly distinguish one from the other—looked at me sternly. In a voice that sounded like a prosecutor's he asked, "How can you remember all that?"

"Well, I was there," I answered.

"No," he persisted. "I mean the dates, the hours and so forth. Since you were blindfolded much of the time and kept alone except for Mr. Tracy, how could you tell one day from another, much less from one week, or one month, or even one year?"

"Well, I'm pretty good with numbers," I said, lightheartedly. Then, in a more serious tone, I tried to explain that I had used a fairly simple mnemonic device, not unlike that of a convict who scratches a mark on the wall of his cell to remind him of the number of days that he has been held a prisoner. The only difference was that the convict knows that when he reaches a certain number, his sentence is completed and he will be released. Since I hadn't been convicted of anything, other than that I was an American in Beirut in the midst of a fierce international struggle, I had no idea of when, or if ever, I would be free again. But keeping track of the days and months and years of captivity was one of the exercises I had used to keep my mind occupied, my sanity intact. It had helped to make me feel that I was still a part of the free world, that I actually existed. And on the day I was released I knew that I had spent one thousand, nine hundred and eight days as a hostage. I had counted every one and kept it in my mind.

One thing I desperately needed at Wiesbaden was dental work. Imagine going for over five years without so much as a dental checkup and being deprived of toothpaste and a good, firm brush.

But Weisbaden had an excellent staff of odontologists, surgeons and technicians, and they went right to work. One remarked on how amazing it was that my teeth had held up as well as they had after all those years, especially on a poor and limited diet. I believe it was because I had never allowed myself to sink totally into despair. I had found that powerful inner strength, the strong will to survive that resides within all of us. This is a kind of holistic medicine and combined with sincere faith and prayer it can make you almost indestructible.

On the second evening in Weisbaden at the hospital, people began to enter my room to inform me that a very special call was coming from the White House, from the President of the United States, George Bush. I picked up the telephone, and to my surprise, it was the President, welcoming me to freedom and saying that all America was awaiting my return. On behalf of Mrs. Bush and himself and all of America, he was calling to praise me and the other hostages for our endurance and safe return. He also informed me that Terry Anderson had been released and was caught up in a snowstorm on his way to Damascus. That meant that all American hostages were on their way home. I thanked him for his concern, but in truth, I was so taken by the event, I was speechless for words, and it was over before I could compose myself.

I was lying in my room when my wife entered with a broad grin on her face. "I have a surprise for you, Joe. Your family is here. They're waiting to see you."

"My family?" I was incredulous. "Oh my God, let me straighten up first." And then they all trooped into the room. My brother Thomas rushed over to me, his eyes brimming with tears, and threw his arms around me in a long brotherly embrace.

"I told them I was going to give you a big hug the moment I saw you," he said. And then he stepped back and looked at me slowly and carefully.

"How do you feel, Joe?" he said. I could hear the concern in his voice.

"I feel wonderful, Thomas," I said. "How do *you* feel?

We all laughed and then I was surrounded by love and affection. My son Eric, who is 25, had read everything he could find about the Middle East during the years I was a hostage and could probably tell me a few things. But boy, could I tell him about Robin Hood and Jane Eyre!

David, who is 32 and a computer programmer, had worked long, hard hours to succeed in his profession but had given every spare moment he had to working for my release. Before he left the States for Wiesbaden, a reporter asked him what he expected when we were reunited and he said, "I don't know. I never had a hostage father before." David is a great kidder and a wonderful young man.

Then there was my sister-in-law, Frances, whom I adore. Frances had worked as hard as anyone in the family for my freedom. She said, "We all wanted to show Joseph that we really cared and we all were working to get him free."

With a support group like that, with their constant efforts, their faith and their prayers, how could I have not have survived?

Elham had remained quietly in the background while we all embraced each other, until I saw her standing there, a soft, happy smile on her face, and brought her into the gathering. There was a concentration of love in that room that I don't think has ever been surpassed in the world. Surely no one has ever been happier than I was at that moment. Now I truly felt that I had rejoined the world of the living.

We were all asked to stand out on the hospital balcony

for a family portrait and to answer some reporters' questions. Thomas nudged me as we were going out and said, "I'm used to this Joe, I've been doing it for five-and-a-half years." At first I was surprised to hear this. I had always thought of Tom as kind of laid-back, a man who rarely wasted words. There is a boyish shyness about him, and yet he had found the courage to face batteries of reporters, to appear repeatedly in television interviews, and to allow armies of photographers and writers to invade his home without ever refusing to answer a question. He was the most powerful spokesman on my behalf in America, as Elham was in the Middle East.

Finally, the doctors gave me a summary of my medical examinations. "You're as good as you feel, Joseph," they told me. "That blow on the head they gave you when you were first abducted may cause a little speech difficulty for a time. The frostbite you suffered on the balcony that winter is permanent, I'm afraid, and will mean a little discomfort now and then, but if anyone can live with it, I'm sure you can. Otherwise you're in remarkable physical condition considering all that you've been through."

The doctors seemed to be as happy with their findings as I was, but still none of them was able to come up with a reason for the strange operation I had undergone in a secret Beirut hospital such a short time before.

Later, a surgeon in America suggested that my condition had been diverticulitis, and explained that it was sort of the opposite of an appendix attack. But to me it will always remain a mystery. What I am sure of is that, without the gentle care and concern of the surgeon who performed the operation, I would not be alive today. It was as though I had been in the hands of God.

Now a doctor smiled at me and said, "Well, Joseph, you're in great shape. How would you like to go home? There are a lot of people waiting to greet you."

"A lot of people?" I said. "Most of my family is already here."

"I'm talking about America, Joe," he said. "The country can't wait to welcome you home."

I looked at him in disbelief. I was still not convinced that there could possibly be anyone interested in me, outside of my friends and family. I would prove to be very mistaken.

"Well, great," I said. "When can I leave?"

"How about tomorrow?" someone asked. "There's a United Airlines jet ready to receive you and your whole family. All you have to do is pack up and leave."

They had been wonderful to me at Wiesbaden but I couldn't get out of there fast enough and be on my way back to America. "We're sad but happy to see you go, Mr. Cicippio," one of the nurses said. And then she put on her stern, professional face and added. "Now you take good care of yourself!"

The day before I was to go home, Alann Steen arrived with his family and we all got together for a joyous visit. I couldn't help thinking of how poorly he looked; of course, he was probably thinking the same about me.

The next day, Alann and I met with Terry Anderson— the last of the American hostages to be released—who had just been flown to Wiesbaden.

A lot has been written about the vacant stare of soldiers who have just returned from heavy combat. We had been through a different kind of war, but I think all three of us recognized something in our expressions that told us we had shared the same fate: one of prolonged misery, loneliness, and deprivation. I had never met Alann or Terry Anderson before, but it was as if I had known them all my life.

The three of us embraced and then we sat and quietly talked about a few of our experiences. Our families were there, and stood watching us in a kind of respectful silence, but it was as though we were alone, locked together in some terrible dark room of captivity. We said very little; speech wasn't necessary. Each of us knew what the other had fought against and overcome.

There is something almost indefinable that separates a human being who has been held in long captivity from others who have not. Sometime later, at a convention in Miami, I saw a man who looked at me with that captive's stare. He approached me and without a word being spoken we embraced. It turned out that he had been a prisoner for long years in a German concentration camp.

Terry told us about the difficulties he had had on the day of his release. His car, being driven from the Baaka Valley to

Damascus, had been caught in a snowdrift in the mountains and his arrival had been delayed by several hours.

"I know what you were thinking, Terry," I said.

"What's that?" he asked.

"You were thinking, Isn't this ever going to end? Is it for real?" Then I told him of my long ride to Damascus when we had been held up by the Election Day celebration. I asked him why he had been held for so long.

"Who knows? Maybe I write too well. Or too poorly!"

Again we laughed quietly, and then he asked, "What about you?"

"Well, I had just raised the students' tuition fee at the university. I might have thought twice about that."

We looked at Alann Steen. "Gave out too many D's, I guess. Not enough A's."

We all laughed again. I don't think our families could understand what we found so amusing, considering that we had all spent so many years in captivity. But a little humor has a way of easing the pain of even the worst experience. Charlie Chaplin wrote that all humor is based on tragedy. I think he was right. If we aren't able to discover the comic absurdity of the most difficult moments in our lives, how unendurable we make it for ourselves.

When a doctor came in and asked us all to appear on the balcony for yet another press conference, we went out together, hand in hand, three families who had survived about the worst that life could inflict on us. I was together with Elham and my family, Alann Steen with his wife, and Terry Anderson with Madeleine and his daughter whom he had never seen until moments before. She had been born while Terry was a captive, and was now six years old.

We three families posed on the balcony steps waving to a small but cheering crowd. It was nothing like what we would confront when we returned to our home towns. There would be more cameras pointed at us, more shouted questions, and an outpouring of affection that I don't think any of us could possibly have imagined.

After the balcony session we all said our goodbyes. Our families were united in a common feeling of affection and understanding. In a sense they had been held prisoners as

much as we had. And each of us—Alann, Terry, and I—
knew it and were very grateful for their support. I can imagine
what it might have been like if we had been totally
abandoned. Even in my darkest moments, when I felt that
the world had truly passed me by, I knew that I lived in the
thoughts of every member of my family. I honestly believe
that without their support, their hopes and prayers, I could
not possibly have survived the long purgatory Hezbollah
had imposed on me.

A hospital official approached me. "Well, it's time to
leave, Mr. Cicippio. Are you all packed up and ready to go?"

"Are you serious?" I asked. "I started packing up five-and-
a-half years ago, but I never got anywhere!"

It didn't take long for all of us to stow our gear in the
cars that were waiting to drive us to the airport. Thomas, his
wife Frances, and my sons had all spent the night in
handsome apartments on the grounds of the medical center,
and had been treated with great regard. It was as though the
people at Wiesbaden knew the pain we had all suffered and
simply couldn't do enough to make our visit there as
comfortable as possible. And they went a long way past
providing just ordinary comfort.

I heard that when Edward Tracy arrived there he was
asked what he would like more than anything in the world
and he said, "A Big Mac and a Coke!" That's exactly what
they served up to him. How they managed to whip that up
in such a short time I don't know, but they did, with all the
trimmings, and I understand that Edward downed it with
great enthusiasm. When you've been deprived of such simple
pleasures for so many years they become things that, quite
frankly, you lust for.

The ride to the airport was swift and smooth and we
were all in a celebrative mood. But I don't think any of us
anticipated the reception the airline had arranged for us. If
we had been a royal family, we couldn't have been greeted
with more fanfare.

The first class compartment had been reserved for us and
a flight attendant popped open a bottle of champagne
only minutes after we were airborne. The food was
sumptuous, the service was constant, there wasn't anything

we could ask them for that they wouldn't try to do.

"Why all the fuss?" I asked a flight attendant.

She smiled sweetly. "Mr. Cicippio, to us you're a hero. We just want to repay you, in a small way, for all the years you spent as a hostage for your country."

Elham nudged me and said, "Joseph, you'd better get used to the idea."

A hero? Certainly I was not. I was only an American businessman who had been taken off the campus of a university in Beirut and had spent more than five years in captivity trying to learn how to survive. The real heroes, in my mind, were my wife Elham, my brother Thomas, and all the members of my family who were so steadfast in their efforts to see me a free man again.

But the flight to America was a great trip and we enjoyed every moment of it. I have flown all over the world on the finest airlines, but I could never have imagined anything as magnificent as that flight.

I sat with Thomas and my sons in the lounge compartment and asked about the news from home. Thomas told me about our sister, Helen.

"You know, Joseph," he said, "The doctors told Helen last June that she had two months to live, but I guarantee you she'll be there when we get to my house in Norristown. She can't wait to see you."

And then my son David, said, "Dad, as sick as she is, she's so full of energy. And she said she'd never give up until she saw you home again."

Eric said, "When she heard you were released she was really excited. 'It's just like I was hugging the whole world, the whole world!' she told everybody. She really loves you, Dad."

They told me how the family had stayed up through the night waiting to hear that I was officially released. It wasn't until 4:07 a.m. that the State Department had called to say I was actually free. Then the family had talked with some reporters who were also keeping a vigil, after which they asked for some privacy.

The Pastor of the King of Peace Church in south Philadelphia was there, and he led the whole family in a prayer on my behalf—a prayer of hope and thanksgiving.

"I would never have made it without your prayers, I'm certain of that," I told them.

"Well, you know Joseph, when we saw you on television that day we were really troubled. Helen has been more concerned about your health than her own," Thomas said. "And that other time when you made that hostage statement, I wasn't even sure it was you. I was so shook up I had to leave the room."

I thanked them all for standing by me, but then I knew my family and never really expected anything else. I told them how truly blessed I was to have such loving support.

We talked for hours on that airplane; there was so much to learn about. I felt like Rip Van Winkle, coming back after five years of being totally out of it. I listened with amazement to all the changes that had taken place in the world.

The Berlin Wall was down. The end of the Cold War was approaching. Fax machines were new and almost commonplace in businesses. Junk bonds were dead. But one of the biggest surprises would come later when I learned that many of my married friends now had two wage earners in their families. When I had left it had been almost unheard-of for a wife to enter the work force.

Finally, we were approaching the airport in Philadelphia. I looked out the window and saw that the city was ablaze in light.

"Why are all the office buildings lit up like that?" I asked innocently. We all went to the windows for a look. It was truly spectacular, like VJ day all over again.

"Must be something special going on," I said.

I still couldn't believe it had anything to do with our arrival.

Then Thomas said, "I think it's for you, Joe. I think they're saying 'Welcome home.'" I shook my head in disbelief.

"Can't be," I murmured.

But it was true. Frank "Hank" Ciaccio, a longtime friend from my hometown of Norristown, had arranged through the Philadelphia Electric Company for all the businesses in town to leave their lights on to celebrate my return. One skyscraper had lettered with lights the words, "Welcome home, Joseph Cicippio," in neon lights.

I was stunned.

After we landed, Senator Harris Wofford of Pennsylvania came aboard with a warm message of greeting from his senate colleagues. In the following days, I would receive remarkable gifts from people I never dreamed had the least concern for my existence. One was Lawrence Coughlin, a member of the House of Representatives from Pennsylvania, who presented me with an American flag that had flown over the Capitol in Washington, D.C. Another was Senator Mark Hatfield, who had written a book called *From a Hard Rock to a Hard Place*, one of the books I was given in captivity. I had found it very inspirational and had mentioned it in one of my interviews. When we met some time later, we had a wonderful talk and shared a quiet moment of prayer together.

But now I was at the airport, and stunned by our reception. It seemed as if everyone I knew was there. One of them was my lawyer and old friend, Skip Oliver, who had stood by me in good times and bad. I will always be grateful for his unflagging devotion.

A battery of cameras was trained on us and reporters shouted questions like machine-gun fire. A representative from Mayor Rendall's office, together with an aide from Governor Casey's office, welcomed us to Philadelphia.

A large bouquet of flowers was thrust into my arms as we were led to a motorcade of limousines. People called out encouragement. I heard "Welcome home, Joe" over and over again. It was though I was a personal friend of every one of them, and their concern for my well-being was very touching.

Thousands of people kept waving and cheering as the motorcade wended its way toward Norristown. When we got there I was stunned all over again. Hundreds of people were waiting for us! The TV camera lights lit up the streets. Reporters lined the sidewalks and stood in clusters on the lawn. When we left the car, a cheer went up and we heard the same cries of sympathy and affection.

I was overwhelmed. I had thought that the American people might be mildly interested in my fate, but I would learn that millions had been praying for me, hoping for me, through all the years of my captivity. My visit to Norristown was just one example of this outpouring of love. In the weeks and months to come I was recognized everywhere and greeted with incredible warmth. I had imagined that a handful of people would know who I was but, once again, I couldn't have been more mistaken. Yellow ribbons were tied to trees and the front doors of homes everywhere, not just for me, of course, but for all the hostages.

The people proved again that we are the most caring nation in the world; we do not forget our own.

We posed for the cameras and answered questions until we were exhausted. We finally pleaded weariness and the need for a good night's rest, and they graciously let us go. We went into the house and there was my sister Helen, waiting for me. "Joseph!" she cried and threw her arms around my neck. We held each other for long, tearful moments.

When I asked about her health she would say only, "Joseph, all the medicines and treatments the doctors gave me weren't anywhere near as good as the thought that I would see you again someday. I wouldn't let myself die."

This brave and strong-willed lady passed away not long after I returned to America. A day doesn't go by when her memory and the memory of my sister, Rose, and my son, Joseph, aren't fixed in my mind.

The family had a few quiet moments together, happy and grateful to be united once again, before we went off to bed.

The next morning it was the same thing all over again—reporters, TV cameras, and people waiting to greet us.

I went out and examined the ingenious display my brother Tom had erected on his front lawn to keep media attention focused on the plight of the hostages. There was David Jacobsen's name, Terry Anderson, Tom Sutherland—all the hostages—with the number of days each was kept in captivity. Under Lt. Col. Higgins's name were two crossed American flags. His sign was edged in black.

I looked at my name with a sign over it that read "Free At Last," and the number of days, 1,908. I marveled at how patient Thomas had been, going out each night to change the numbers. But then Thomas has always been a very patient man. It also reminded me of the great love and concern my brother has for me.

Several months later, Robert Polhill, the Beirut University College teacher who had been taken hostage, agreed to come to Norristown and help us to ceremoniously dismantle the display, even though he was recovering from his throat cancer. He said, "The signs are a symbol of the many supporters who could have shrugged us off and done nothing." Then he added, "Joe and I and the others owe a debt of gratitude to all who remembered."

Students in schools from all over the area came to participate in the ceremony. Some kids from the Norristown High School came and stood right alongside the professional cameramen and filmed the event for their student TV program.

I made a brief statement: "I have always said someone above was looking out for me, and after last week, if we were still being held, none of us would be alive." That was the week when a squadron of Israeli helicopters ambushed a convoy of cars in southern Lebanon and killed Abbas Musawi, Secretary-General of the Hezbollah and greatly revered by the followers of the Islamic Jihad. Once again the Israeli strategy backfired. The result was a new outpouring of fervent support for Hezbollah, the strongest ever seen in Lebanon. If I had still been held when this event took place, I don't think I would have lived for a week. Nor would Alann Steen or Terry Anderson. Every hostage still being held would have felt the wrathful vengeance of the Hezbollah.

During the ceremony, Tom's grandson, Justin Suita, led all the students there in reciting No Greater Love's pledge of peace. It was a moving recital. Together they said: "I hereby commit myself to fostering peace." (No Greater Love is an organization that works to support families of hostages, and families who have lost loved ones in wars or acts of violence.) After the signs were taken down, Thomas donated them to the group. The founder and chairwoman of No Greater Love, Caremella LaSpada, said they would be displayed in Washington as an educational demonstration for peace.

My sign was the last to come down, and Thomas helped me remove it. We held it for a few moments before giving it to a small boy standing there. Tom and I embraced and he said, "Thank God it's over. But you know, I'm going to miss all the great friends we've made in the media. Many's the night they slept right here, on our doorstep."

But I know that Thomas was glad that things would soon return to normal; there would be no more press conferences, no more interviews, no more telephone calls to jar him out of sleep in the middle of the night. For the last time the reporters and cameramen would crowd around him, thrusting microphones into his face. I don't think he misses it, but while it was going on he handled it with as much ease and toughness as was humanly possible to do. Thomas showed a side that I never knew existed and I will always remember him for it.

I've often thought, "What a wonderful brother I have. What a wonderful family." All of them were willing to do anything they could to see me free and safe again. In a lighthearted way, Thomas had vowed never to eat a dish of ice cream, his favorite dessert, until I could share one with him. And we did, right there on the front lawn of his home.

Chapter 26

Joseph: The attention that I received at home the first week was overwhelming. Constant media attention and continuous visitors left me with little time to think, or just relax. I was contacted by my lawyer, Skip Oliver, who asked if I would like a ride through Valley Forge Park. Elham and I immediately accepted.

It was a crisp winter day in December, but certainly not cold. As we walked through the park with its leafless trees and looked out over the open space, I mentioned to Skip my dream of visiting the Tournament of Roses and Rose Bowl Parade. I told him that the scent of flowers was so real I could actually smell them, and I wanted Elham to experience this yearly extravaganza. It was one of the promises that I had made to myself during my five years of captivity—one day visiting Pasadena and the Tournament of Roses Parade with Elham.

The following day Skip Oliver was on the phone to the Pasadena Visitors Bureau, first speaking to wonderful Mary Ausloos and then to the executive director, Gail Thompson, setting in motion what would be one of the greatest experiences of my life. Skip explained to Gail Thompson and to Bill Flinn, her colleague at the Tournament of Roses, how during my captivity, I had often thought of fulfilling my long-held dream of Elham and I attending the Parade of Roses and Rose Bowl Game in Pasadena. When I was freed, it was one of my first wishes. It was not our intention to impose, but simply to ascertain if we could acquire accommodations and the necessary tickets. The Tournament of Roses Committee's enthusiasm in having us attend was heartwarming. Apparently, they immediately received the concurrence of Bob Cheney, president of the Tournament of Roses, and plans were set in motion for our attendance.

The Committee had already had two grand marshals,

those being Ben "Knighthorse" Campbell, now a United States Senator, and Christo Columbus, a direct descendent of the famous explorer. We were being invited as special guests.

We arrived on Sunday, December 29, 1991, and were taken to the Pasadena Hilton Hotel and met by Gail Thompson. She, Mary Ausloos, and Skip Oliver had talked so often on the telephone that they greeted each other as old friends. It was then that I met our personal escort, Bob Johnson and his wonderful wife, Penny. They were our constant companions throughout our visit and have remained dear friends.

We were the guests of the Johnsons for dinner, and I could hardly rest that evening in anticipation of the excitement to follow.

The following morning, Monday, December 30, 1991, Elham and I were picked up at the Pasadena Hilton Hotel by Bob Johnson and his wife, and Elham, Skip, and I were driven to the interview room of the Grand Marshall's Room of the Tournament of Roses Building. The building is the former Wrigley mansion of Wrigley chewing gum fame.

After spending the morning in interviews, we met with the queen and her court, the grand marshals, the tournament president and the mayor of Pasadena. After lunch we were taken to the bandfest held at the Pasadena City College, featuring six of the best marching bands that were participating in the Rose Bowl Parade. I walked in with my wife, Elham, and Skip. My introduction was overwhelming to me—tears came to my eyes. As a former drum major, the bandfest had a strong impact on me. I was just overwhelmed by hearing and watching those wonderful marching bands. After spending almost five years in isolation, I finally felt alive, and it was exhilarating to feel those life-giving juices flow again.

That evening we were picked up for the Tournament of Roses Director's Dinner at the Ritz-Carlton, which was a black tie affair. It was truly a special event as invitations were restricted. It was a privilege to be a special guest with others that included the officials of the Pac 10 and Big 10, ABC Television Sports, and the Tournament of Roses director. The presidents of both universities and the president of the

Tournament were also in attendance and spoke. I was introduced and, graciously, not asked to speak. The dinner was the most prestigious event to lead up to the parade and game. It was the first time that Bob Johnson, who had spent almost thirty years with the Tournament of Roses, and his wife, Penny, were invited to attend.

The following day we visited several of the areas where the floats were being built. Elham and I saw first-hand how all of the flowers were applied in a last minute frenzy in preparation for the big day. The famous Rose Bowl float construction was particularly exciting for Elham, as she was asked to help build one of the floats, placing some flowers in the construction frame. The aroma was magnificent, and seeing the colorful flowers making various designs was overwhelming. The float construction would continue the last twenty-four hours before the parade, with shifts around the clock to perfect the designs. There was something for everyone to do, the young and old, the able and the disabled, men and women working in harmony to complete their floats.

We were then whisked off to the Kiwanis Kick-off Luncheon held at the Pasadena Convention Center. There I met ABC Television officials, and university officials, including the presidents and athletic directors, coaches and selected team members, who were introduced to the media and to approximately 3,500 attendees. It was a gala luncheon and you could feel the excitement for the Rose Bowl game which was to take place the following day.

That evening, December 31, 1991, was my first New Year's Eve in over five years to be spent with my wife, Elham. It was especially nice to share it with Judy and Skip Oliver, my old friends, as guests at the Pasadena Holiday Inn. Judy Haismann, director of sales and marketing made it an especially wonderful evening. All of the guests in attendance made me feel at home. As midnight approached, tears welled in all of our eyes, and I truly knew this was going to be the happiest New Year.

Having been freed of my chains, everything was coming up roses.

The next morning I was like a small child, eagerly looking

forward to the parade. I was as much excited for Elham as I was for myself. I knew that she would be overwhelmed by the beauty and artistry that went into the creation of the floats and into the spectacular arrangements of the floral designs that mark each display. After a brief interview with ABC Television on Colorado Avenue, the Tournament of Roses Parade began, with Elham and I sitting on the official reviewing stand. It truly was a spectacular sight. The air was rich with the fragrance of freshly cut flowers. Beauty surrounded us. The parade was everything I expected it to be and more. It lasted approximately two hours, and we were then taken to the Rose Bowl, where the Tournament of Roses luncheon was served. The excitement and the spectacle of the parade will always be indelibly imprinted in my mind.

After the luncheon I was invited to the University of Washington locker room by head coach, Don James. I had lost approximately thirty-five pounds and was still somewhat weak from my ordeal. At approximately 138 pounds, I was amazed at the sight of those magnificent athletes, who were in top physical condition.

Then, there we were—at the 78th Rose Bowl Game. I had the distinct honor of tossing the coin in mid-field which pitted the University of Washington Huskies against the University of Michigan Wolverines. It was the first American football game that Elham had ever seen. It was a spectacular game, the University of Washington becoming the Rose Bowl victors. Skip and I rooted for the University of Washington because my host was part of the Pac 10, and Elham and her friend, Judy, rooted for the University of Michigan in the Big 10.

The following day, January 2, 1992, I attended the post-parade viewing of the floats, and in a way, it was more spectacular than seeing them the first time, since now you could leisurely stroll while the floats were in view for all to see. Bob and Penny's daughter gave Elham and me a personal tour of one of the floats, and it was amazing to see how intricate the floats were designed and how they were driven through Pasadena with very little road visibility.

Our trip to wonderful California concluded with being

honored guests at the Universal Studios in Hollywood. My special thanks to Patricia "P.J." Sherban, who was my host, and who made it a wonderful and pleasurable experience. It was truly a pleasure to see what Hollywood had to offer and how they could "make believe." The tour of Universal Studios was a magnificent final touch to the great California visit.

I truly want to express my sincere appreciation for the kind and generous attention shown to me by all those wonderful people in Pasadena who were responsible for making my dream come true. I shall always remember the kindness shown to me by all of the members of the Pasadena Tournament of Roses Association. To my dying day, I shall always be grateful.

Before leaving Pasadena, I managed to have lunch at Malone's Pub in Pasadena with two former hostages, Dave Jacobson and Father Jenco. Dave and Father Jenco related some of their stories while in captivity. They were held with Anderson and Sutherland and laughed at how they were able to watch television and see some American shows. We laughed as Dave Jacobson spoke of bribing the guards and talked them into getting ice cream for them. We joked about how when they were to be released they would be too old to work, and they would market a "hostage kit" with makeup items like Preparation H, blindfolds, toilet paper, etc. I was truly amazed at all of this because I had rarely received coffee, had no television, had not been allowed to talk, and had had to read by candlelight.

When leaving Pasadena Elham talked about our wonderful experiences. She was thinking about all of the poor, orphaned children in war-torn Lebanon who had never seen such wonder or such beauty. The following year, Elham and I, along with many volunteers went about arranging to bring children from orphanages in Beirut to the United States for Christmas. We were able to raise approximately one hundred thousand dollars through private and corporate donations, and make arrangements with the Lebanese government to have the children flown into the United States.

We brought over thirty-two orphaned children from various faiths—Christian, Muslim, and Druse. When we greeted them at the Newark International Airport, you could see the pain in their eyes. A terrible sixteen-year-old war had left its mark on all of them. Of the eighteen girls, one of them, Carmen Khoukassian, echoed my own feelings when she said, "I love all the religions. It is the same God, because he is our creator." This from a fourteen-year-old child, who had endured bombings and gunfire all of her life, and yet emerged with what I feel is an expression of truth, faith, and love.

Elham and I again experienced the wonderful Rose Bowl and Tournament of Roses Parade, only this time we shared it with children who would return to the Arab world with memories of a wonderful experience in America.

Chapter 27

Elham: As a native of Lebanon who grew up in Beirut and witnessed sixteen years of war, I was taken by the joy, the wonderful spirit of Christmas, and the magic events in Pasadena, and at the same time feeling a sorrow deeply inside me for the Lebanese children who had been born during the war and never had the chance to enjoy the beauty of the world. Impulsively, I said: "I wish I could enjoy what I am experiencing here, but there are too many innocent children left behind with no hope and no future, their only sin being born in a country at war." Those words were the beginning of a new dream.

Officials of the Tournament of Roses, who had observed my deep feelings, later came forward with a proposal to host forty underprivileged Lebanese children at the 1993 Tournament of Roses.

Therefore, with such encouragement, Joseph and I outlined a program to bring those children to the United States of America and show them the magic of our country at Christmastime. We chose children between the ages of nine and fourteen from Lebanese orphanages. Their itinerary included tours of New York; Washington, D.C., which included the White House, The Liberty Bell, and Independence Hall in Philadelphia; Disneyland, Universal Studios, Sea World, and finally, the Tournament of Roses Parade and Rose Bowl in Pasadena, California.

All the children were given medical examinations at the Hahnemann University Hospital, which was the part of their visit that they least enjoyed, although they were treated with great kindness by the staff and doctors. After a while, their vacant, frightened stares all had vanished, and they were laughing and talking together.

The doctors and nurses, knowing how few pleasures they had been treated to in their lives, were almost overly indulgent. The children were given a big American breakfast of pancakes, fruit cup, doughnuts, and warm milk and cocoa, a feast they had rarely enjoyed in their impoverished, war-torn country. The doctors and staff joined with them, even the hospital president and the chief executive officer, Iqbal F. Paroo, one of the most humble, warm, generous persons I have ever met. Iqbal F. Paroo took a genuine personal interest in seeing to the children's medical needs and personal needs.

The children were remarkably alert and knowledgeable. They asked about the helicopters in the hospital's trauma unit. Some asked if they could sit in during a surgical procedure. One even asked about the Chicago Bulls basketball team! How could they possibly have known about such things?

One girl, Ramona Khattar, a fourteen-year-old with wide, doe-like brown eyes in a sweet, soft face surrounded by ringlets, seemed to have a crush on the American actor Jason Priestly. She had seen his show, "Beverly Hills 90210," in Lebanon and yearned to meet him. "Just to say hello," she said quietly.

Ramona, who looked like a typical American teenager in jeans, a sweater, and topsiders, perhaps summed up the experience for all the kids. She said, "I never thought I could come to America. It was a dream, and I don't believe I am here."

All the medical services the children received were donated by the hospital. Nurses, doctors, psychiatrists, and nutritionists had all volunteered their time to help out, and spent many hours to ensure that the kids went home with the most thorough medical reports possible.

In fact, the chairman of the Department of Pediatrics at the hospital, Emanuel Lebenthal, delayed a holiday visit to Israel so he could give his full attention to each and every child. He supervised all the examinations without a thought that some of them might, symbolically, represent enemies of his country.

I wish that such love and concern would prevail in the Middle East and in all the troubled parts of the world. To Lebenthal they were just children, innocent victims of a conflict that is difficult for anyone, of any age, to understand.

If you were to pass by those children on the streets of an American town, you would probably think they were just kids on their way to an outing somewhere. All of them loved Michael Jackson, and so, hospital workers scoured the video stores in the area to pick up one or two videotapes for them. As far as the hospital staff was concerned, there wasn't enough that they could do for the children. And I began to realize that the kids knew more about American pop culture than I ever would.

Dr. Lebenthal announced that the children's health was quite good except that a few were anemic, one had an enlarged liver, and another a heart murmur. But they were all fit to travel with us, and we had arranged for what we hoped would be an exciting tour of the United States for them.

We loved all the children, truly without exception, but one especially captured our hearts. His name is Nicholas Issa, and he had seen his family destroyed by a tank shell. One sister had been beheaded; another was so badly wounded that she was taken to a hospital and, as he says, "put to sleep." Little Nicholas suffered body wounds and lost an arm. He remembers all of this horror, although he was less than three years old at that time. Nicholas's father was killed on the spot.

What an appealing child he is, and how bravely he has endured the tragedy of his life. I was determined that Nicholas would stay with us until he had been fitted with the very finest prosthetic device that Dr. Frank Malone could provide. Funding for the prosthesis was organized by Janet Maalouf, wife of the Lebanese chargé d'affaires, through the board of trustees of the St. Jude Hospital. The members of the board paid for the artificial arm themselves. And again, Iqbal Paroo, who himself had lost his leg at an early age, made this his project with us.

We kept Nicholas Issa for an additional two weeks to fit him for a prosthetic device. It occurred to me that the first doctors to examine him were an Israeli, Emanuel Lebenthal, and two Egyptians, Mahmood Alasmi and Ali Hani, who were able to talk to those children whose English was imperfect. They had showed only kindness and caring for the children and sincere respect for each other. It showed me what humanity can achieve if there is less hatred and bitterness.

Nicholas was amazingly adept. He was fitted with both an artificial arm and a hook device, which he actually preferred, since it gave him more flexibility. In no time, he was using it with as much skill and dexterity as if it had been his real arm. How proud I am of him and how brave I think he is. His courage and spirit are so big you hardly see the rest of him.

We felt a kind of emptiness when Nicholas had to return to his country, but I think he will always remember the love that we, and many others, felt for him. I know that he will always remain in our memory and prayers.

We managed to obtain a few cameras, and the children never stopped taking pictures of everything they saw and of each other. Picture-taking was fascinating to them, even more than Disneyland, where they were treated to just about every ride. And the cameras never stopped clicking. They spent about all of their allowances on film.

It was a glorious trip, and wonderful to see how happily the children responded. Their eyes had lost that empty, frightened look and now were shining with hope for the future. It was not only a healing process for the kids, but for Joseph and for me.

It may sound strange to those who think of such things as ordinary, even as a chore, but one of the highlights of the children's visit was a shopping tour of the King of Prussia Mall in Pennsylvania. They were dazzled by the Rose Bowl Parade, the trip to Disneyland, Universal Studios, and all of the sights they had seen in New York City, but an afternoon walking through a typical American shopping center left them almost speechless with wonder. It made me realize again how blessed we are in this country and how much we tend to take such seemingly mundane things for granted.

With the cooperation of United Airlines; Middle East Airline; Academy Bus Tours; The Scanticon Hotel in Princeton, New Jersey; The Holiday Inn in Pasadena, California; The American Embassy in Beirut; our friend Mrs.

Sayegh from the American University in Beirut, who had spent days making arrangements with all the orphanages; Hahnemann Hospital, Philadelphia, Pennsylvania; The Pasadena Convention and Visitor Bureau, California, and The Pasadena Center, California; and the Pasadena Tournament of Roses, California, we were able to accomplish this project.

Joseph was determined to accomplish the project at any price. I remember, prior to the arrival of the children, we were short of money by twenty-five thousand dollars. We were facing a deadline for payment of the airline tickets. I had suggested canceling the project for the year and working it out the following year. Joseph looked straight into my eyes saying, "How dare you even think that way? Isn't it enough to be an orphan? What would happen to you if someone promised you a trip to America, and at the last minute told you that the trip was cancelled? These children are coming no matter what, and we are going to fulfill our promise. Have faith, Elham!" Joseph said.

"I have faith, but we need money," I replied. Again, Joseph looked at me and said, "Have faith first and last, and God will help us."

There were a lot of tears—sad but happy tears—when it came time to say goodbye to the kids, but they had been allowed to see a part of America that might give them some feeling of how beautiful life can be. We truly believe what a famous poet once said: "A thing of beauty is a joy forever." We were blessed by bringing joy to the eyes of those innocent children who have had such a devastating life living in a war-torn country from the day they were born. Even if it was only for a short period of time, our message was to plant hope in their lives. One little thirteen-year-old girl, Samar Samaha said, "I hope the future will be good. War is terrible."

Chapter 28

Joseph: My life had been in limbo for five years, but now it was almost unreal. I had never expected the response of the American people to my homecoming. I was greeted at airports, toasted at dinners, and invited on speaking tours of schools, churches, and universities.

I was welcomed to the White House on a couple of occasions. Whatever your politics are, let me assure you that the Bush family is a warm and loving group, each supportive of each other. The president and his wife couldn't have been kinder to me and to the other former hostages who met with them. I don't think it was politics that motivated them; I think they had a genuine concern for our safety and well-being.

If there was one jarring moment on my return, it was that the American University of Beirut did not exactly welcome me back with a warm embrace and some assurances about my future.

I believe I worked for them with as much dedication as I have for anyone I have ever been employed by, and yet when I got home, they first told me to rest, and later, that there was no room for me in the organization. How naive I had been. During the long painful years of my captivity, I never doubted that I would remain a member of the university staff. During my captivity I was even thinking of how to improve the university. I spent much time and thought on the creation of a school of banking, to be the first such school in the entire Middle East. Over the years I had thoroughly worked out the smallest details for the entire program. I had spent many hours on ideas to resolve the university's financial problems. They made an almost laughable suggestion that I return to the University in Beirut, knowing perfectly well that I would refuse. I was simply cast adrift.

The prospect of having to begin my career all over again was not too reassuring. I wasn't a young, brash, eager kid anymore. But the lessons I had learned as a hostage had taught me not to despair. That would have been too easy. Again, I searched within myself for the wellspring of strength that had helped me to survive the hostage years. I was not about to quit then, not after all Elham and my family had been through.

One of the great pleasures I had had after returning to this country was to walk through the aisles of a supermarket in New Jersey. It wasn't just to shop, although it was a delight to be able to remove from the shelves whatever struck my fancy, check the price, read the contents of the item, and return it if I wasn't satisfied. So many people in the world don't have that freedom of choice. But what was more enjoyable for me was simply being among the people, free and unthreatened. Without trying to snoop, I listened to their small talk, the kind of conversations Americans exchange every day of their lives. I found it so refreshing. It made me feel more and more like a free man in a free country.

I tried to remain as inconspicuous as possible, but the day arrived when I was recognized. Andy Warhol said that everyone is famous for fifteen minutes, but I had thought my moment in the limelight was over. The market deli manager pointed me out and said, "You know who that is? That's Joe Cicippio," and my anonymity was gone. On my next visit a local press photographer took a photograph of me wheeling a cart from the parking lot. A reporter waited for me with a pad full of questions. I had come to grips with the idea that I wasn't going to be an ordinary citizen again, at least not for a while.

"Why are you doing the shopping, Mr. Cicippio?" the reporter asked, as though I was doing something unmanly.

"It's part of the therapy," I told her. "Coming back to the world after being out of it for so long." It was the best answer I could think of. It wasn't altogether wrong, but I might have said that I just like to shop.

They even listed my purchases when I was at the checkout counter: sour cream, a pint of half-and-half, parsley, strawberries, a loaf of bread, a prime rib. I hoped they wouldn't think I was some kind of hedonist!

I have no quarrel with the press, though. They helped to keep me in the public eye when I might easily have been forgotten, and they wrote many supportive articles about the plight of the hostages. There was no reporter or interviewer I turned away, because I think the story I had to tell was important, not just to the American people, but to people everywhere.

If I wanted to emulate anyone with regard to my dealings with the media, it was my brother, Thomas. He had been told that too much attention to those of us who were held might be playing into the hands of our captors. Tom thought otherwise. If the people hadn't been constantly reminded that there were innocent men out there whose lives were in danger, nothing would have been done. One American official, who was completely stymied about how to "cut a deal" for the hostages' release, actually said that the best thing might be for everyone to pretend that we had all been killed in an accident—and to forget us. Of course, he wasn't a hostage. He didn't have a son, a brother, or a father living in misery and loneliness, with the very intense, moment-to-moment feeling that his life was imperiled.

When it was suggested to Tom that it might be best for him to tone down his day-to-day protest about the hostage situation, he just smiled and turned away. "Look," he said, "it has to be done. My brother has lost his freedom, and I'm not going to let people in this country forget it. I'm still an American and I can talk to anyone I wish."

But Thomas did it with restraint. He made people think, "What if that were your relative in there, someone you love and care for?" And the people responded, not just for me, but for every hostage whose name appeared on Tom's front-lawn display. Tom cared about all of us. I think his descretion was admirable and his charity and compassion immense.

My love for Tom and for all the millions of people who had a real concern for the hostages extended now to my feelings for the children, who were as much victims of the war as we had been. Love has a way of growing, and without it I think we are lost.

If there was one thing I learned as a captive, it was that I had to remain as active as possible, so I accepted every speaking engagement that was made to me. My message was simple; it might be titled, "The Price of Freedom." I wanted everyone, especially young people, to know that there are times when we have to sacrifice for those things that we find most precious in our lives.

I also tried to stress how important love and forgiveness is in our lives. How hatred and bitterness make too heavy a burden to bear. My own son, David, whom I love deeply, has said, "Maybe my father can forgive his captors, but I never can." David has a warm heart, and I believe that eventually he will come around to my way of thinking.

Another thing that occupied my time was answering the letters of support that I got from all parts of the world. Some were particularly touching. Meredith Thompson in Williamsburg, Virginia, wrote:

"I turned 18 on January 15 and the best present I got was hearing that the bracelet I wore with pride will be forwarded." (Bracelets that pleaded for the hostage's release were worn by many Americans.) "I give all my love and hope to [those] brave men. They will never lose a place in my heart."

Another, from Trish Gaughian, who had worn a bracelet for five years and now had sent it to me, said:

"This bracelet has been a part of my life. All of the hostages have been in my thoughts and prayers, but you and your family have held a special place in my heart. I have waited so long to write this letter. I know the Lord will give you strength, just as you were strong enough to survive your ordeal."

She ended her letter with a blessing for a long, healthy, and *peaceful* life.

Yet another, from Michele Russo in Peekskill, New York, said:

"This is a letter I've waited and prayed to write for many years. It is wonderful for me to know that you are finally free. I'd like to tell you that I was with you in spirit for five years. Many, many people hoped and prayed for you."

These, and hundreds of other letters I received, reminded me of how cynical I had been at times in captivity. How I felt that I had been deserted by my own country, my own people. That was anything but the truth. I don't think there have been any people in any nation in history who showed more love and concern for their fellow countrymen in distress.

One letter stands out in my mind. Shortly after my return, I tried in vain to reach Edward Tracy, who is now a patient at a veteran's facility in Boston. I have spoken to him a few times since, and our first moments of conversation are often hopeful. He sounds lucid and on his way to recovery, but then, without any warning, he descends into the darkness of his mind.

I wrote to his sister, Maria Lambert, offering to do what little I could and asking her to keep me apprised of Edward's condition.

She wrote me back a letter card with a Gaelic blessing on the front of it. "May the road rise to meet you. May the wind always be at your back. May the sun shine warm on your face, the rain fall soft upon your fields, and until we meet again, may Gold hold you in the palm of his hand."

It is a lovely sentiment and I knew it was sincerely meant. But then she went on to write what was, for me, even more moving.

She wrote:

"... hardly a day goes by that I don't think of you and thank God for your presence in my brother's life... Father Jenco says that his saving was his religion, the Bible, and human companionship. I'm sure that your five years with my brother didn't give you the saving grace of companionship. I hope it's of some significance to you that your companionship to [Edward] may have been *his* saving grace."

She went on to say that the family had not really understood Edward's mental condition and that before he returned to the Middle East, after an earlier visit in the 1980's, he had announced that he was going to sever all ties with them.

I thought of the guards who had no more awareness of Tracy's illness than his family had had, and who had subjected him to cruel and merciless persecution. Edward didn't deserve that, and I think that, of all the hostages, he was the most terribly and needlessly punished. His agony endures to this day, and my hope and prayers remain with him.

I have tried to forget the memories of my time in captivity, but that is simply not possible. For the first six months after my release I would find myself awake at 3:00 a.m., to catch up with all the news I had missed.

There were nights when I would cry out, "No, No!" and Elham would have to shake me awake and reassure me that I was no longer a hostage. But as time passed, the episodes of post-traumatic-stress disorder became fewer, and now I'm able to go to bed without worrying that I'll get the "willies" in the middle of the night. No question, though, that the memories will always be there.

What I've tried to do is to look at life in a positive way, both while I was a hostage and since I have been released. The sixty pounds I lost as a captive was a kind of blessing. After all, I was quite overweight on the day I was kidnapped, and I had given serious thought to taking off some pounds. Captivity was a strenuous way to do it, but, boy, did it work!

There is a kind of randomness to fate; none of us can really anticipate what the future has in store for us. And so I admire the many people who have overcome the worst kinds of calamity and refused to surrender. People who have been victims of serious accidents and are confined to wheelchairs, for example, but continue to lead meaningful and productive lives. By comparison with many of those brave souls, the ordeal I experienced was insignificant.

So many people have said to me, "Joseph, how can you not hate those people who took five years from your life? How can you forgive them?" My answer is always that I do it for myself. If I allow myself to descend into unremitting hatred for my captors, which is a kind of despair, I would only be defeating my own humanity. When the great baseball player, Lou Gehrig, gave his farewell address at Yankee Stadium, he said, "Today, I consider myself the luckiest man on the face of the earth." He knew he had only a short time to live, and yet he refused to curse his fate or to lapse into despair and bitterness. I sometimes remembered those words when I was a captive, and I think of them still. How could I surpass such gallantry?

Many of us hostages emerged from captivity far stronger than before we were abducted. Terry Anderson's sister Peggy Say says Terry is a much "softer" person. I believe there is strength in "softness." Alann Steen has learned to adjust to the seizures he now has to endure after having been so severely beaten by one of his captors. Others simply and quietly resumed normal lives.

I wish I hadn't been hit on the head and dragged away at the cost of five years of my life, years that I might have spent happily with my wife and family. I still feel pain in the bones of my hands and feet from time to time and would be happy if it would just go away. Frostbite is something that just doesn't leave you. It is sometimes extremely unpleasant, and yet it is a constant reminder of the struggle I had to endure in order to survive. In a way, it is to me a kind of symbol of the daily agony and loneliness that all the hostages had to live through.

But the real victims are those who didn't make it through that dark night of their lives.

I think of William Buckley, crying out for blueberry pancakes and syrup before he died in his squalid bed. Of Lieutenant Colonel Higgins, surely aware that he was about to meet a fate that ultimately I would find myself resigned to. Also of Dennis Hill shot to death. Of Padfield and Douglas taken out with my dear friend Peter Kilburn and shot to death on a remote beach in Lebanon in reprisal for the bombing of Libya, something of which they were totally innocent, except by association with their nation. And of Alec Collett, the British journalist who was hanged, I believe, because of political muddling and intransigence in the same incident. At that time the lives of all the hostages being held had been placed in peril.

I don't think there is a single captive who didn't think, at one time or another, that he had been abandoned by his country. Except for the support and prayers of the average man and woman, we were expendable. And though the emphasis was always on the Western hostages, hundreds and hundreds were kidnapped and murdered in that country. Their families have tried to discover their whereabouts without success.

When Tom Sutherland was released, his Shiite guard almost apologized to him. He said, "Taking the hostages was a waste of time. We didn't get anything out of it." That isn't quite true. The Iranian government certainly got a considerable quantity of weapons and parts.

But I don't believe the hostage crisis in the Middle East is necessarily over. In fact, shortly after the Israelis assassinated Sheikh Abbas Musawi, the Iranian newspaper *Salan* stated publicly that releasing the Western hostages was a mistake and hinted strongly that the practice of taking hostages might be renewed. There are about three thousand Westerners living in Beirut, including many Americans. I imagine that some of them are looking over their shoulders. I know I did before Elham and I left there.

Today, David Jacobsen and I have a six-hundred-million-dollar lawsuit pending against the Iranian government. We claim that our abductions were orchestrated by Iran in order to recover millions of dollars held in the United States after the U.S. Embassy in Teheran was taken over in 1979 and the American staff held captive for fifteen months.

It isn't the money. No amount could possibly compensate us for the years we spent as captives, or repay our families for the misery they endured. But we figure that by hitting them in the pocket we might prevent them from starting hostage-taking all over again. Several other American hostages have joined in this lawsuit.

After all, there is no real difference between the terrorist actions of the Iranian government and the Lebanese Hezbollah. And despite the efforts of President Rafsanjani to reach some conciliation with the West, there are still plenty of fanatics over there ready to start up again. If Rafsanjani should lose in the political in-fighting that's going on, there's no telling what might happen.

Meanwhile, the jihad continues. Every now and then, Hussein rattles his saber and the West responds by bombing Baghdad. Recently a fierce battle between Israeli troops and the Hezbollah army took place in southern Lebanon. Hardly a day goes by that you don't read of an Israeli attacking a Palestinian or the other way around.

Terrorist attacks have even entered these shores, as in the bombing of the World Trade Center building in New York and the plot to blow up vital areas such as the Holland Tunnel and the United Nations. They are already demonstrating the truth of the old World War II slogan, "It can happen here."

Things have changed in Iran, somewhat, since the election of Hashemi Rafsanjani, but not that much. Islamic fundamentalists still stalk the streets arresting women for wearing sunglasses and men for dressing in T-shirts. Any hint of Western influence is considered criminal.

The Bahais are also being persecuted. In 1991 a secret order called for their dismissal from jobs and universities. When the order became known it was vigorously condemned in the United Nations. The Clinton administration also denounced it, but the mullahs despise Bahais, whom they consider members of a heretical offshoot of Islam. There are about three hundred thousand Bahais in Iran. Where can they go? What recourse do they have?

In fact, they are not even allowed to lie peacefully in death. Recently, the government ordered bulldozers to uproot the bodies in a Bahai cemetery in Teheran to make room for a cultural center.

How can we expect hostilities to ease in the Middle East when there are countries where terrorism is an endemic mind-set?

And so, while I am overjoyed at being a free man in a free country, my mind keeps turning back to the troubled, blood-soaked battlegrounds of the Middle East. I think especially of the children and the other innocent victims of conflicts that seem to have no ending. But I also carry with me a new, unshakable appreciation of the human spirit. Maybe it's necessary to experience the chains before you can learn to truly cherish the roses.

Many questions remain to be answered. What would have happened if the United States had entered open, full-scale negotiations for the hostages within the rule of law? The nations that didn't stonewall in the crisis had hostages released far sooner on average. I wonder, now and then, if a demonstration of force might have had any positive effect, or whether it would have resulted in my death and the death of the other hostages. Those are tough questions and I don't pretend that I'm able to answer them. But should another hostage crisis arise, I hope the free world will be able to respond to it with greater skill and diplomacy.

After a year and a half of seeking regular employment, I was finally rewarded. The Clinton administration invited me to interview for a position with the Agency for International Development. I spoke with them a few times in Washington and was given the position of Deputy Chief of Cash Management and Disbursement. For someone who has always been fascinated with figures and budgets, the job was tailor-made for me, and I love every minute of it. After living in Princeton, New Jersey, where I had expected to commute to employment in New York, we moved to the Washington area and found a lovely home in Arlington, Virginia.

Every day is a new challenge and I face each one with joy and excitement. I've come a long way from a frozen balcony in Beirut.

I have everything to be thankful for: a wonderful wife and family, a job I love, a future that is no longer as uncertain as it was such a short time ago. I even have four new grandchildren who were born while I was a hostage. Like Lou Gehrig, I consider myself the luckiest man on the face of the earth.

I have survived the long journey from chains to roses.